Should Christians
Obey The
Ten Commandments?

by M.V. Baxter

This small work is dedicated
to:

- You, the reader, for yielding your most valuable resource to better understand and apply God's word and will in your life and the lives of others.
- Terry Haynie, my mentor, who will always be more knowledgeable and intelligent than I am, but spent considerable time expounding the Scriptures with me.
- My wife, Dawn, who without complaint took care of many obligations so that I might have the time to author this little book.
- My parents who taught me from a young age to examine God's word for myself and to never trust in the teachings of men.
- The Holy Spirit who prompts and moves me in ways which I may never fully comprehend.
- My Lord, Jesus Christ, who illogically died for my redemption and reconciliation.
- God, the Father, who chose and called a sinful "hypocrite of hypocrites," a hateful and self-righteous man that will never deserve His mercy and lovingkindness.

Special Thanks
to:

Yorke S. Warden

and

Living Stream Ministry

for their generosity and permission
to extensively utilize quotations
from the Recovery Version.

3

Table of Contents

Introduction

I was sitting at my desk one day when a good friend and fellow believer stopped by my office. He's a devout Christian man that started a men's group comprised of both Catholics and Protestants with the intent to bring unity between all Christians in our small county. Obviously, he had earned my admiration and respect.

We discussed several religious topics, but then he caught me completely off guard when he said, *"It really upsets me when I see Christians mowing their lawn on Sunday."* Being surprised, I asked why this troubled him. He explained that Sunday was the Christian Sabbath and faithful Christians should not be working on the Sabbath. We had a brief discussion on the applicability of the Mosaic Law upon Christians, but afterwards I wondered how many other Christians felt or believed the same as my friend.

I found that most Christians who possess a reverence for God's word assume we should obey the Ten Commandments. The question never gets a second thought. We have heard them preached from the pulpits since our youth. We uphold them as our standard, our universal creed to demonstrate our uniqueness from the world. We vehemently protest whenever our government seeks to remove them from our courthouses, schools or any other establishment. We proudly hang them in our homes as a reminder of who we are and what we represent. We faithfully memorize them, and we incite others to know them as well.

If it is, indeed, true that Christians should obey the Ten Commandments, then we need to make sure all believers know this truth. This requirement should be clearly stated and adherence to it must be mandated or believers may jeopardize their own salvation. On the other hand, if obedience to the Mosaic Law is not really required of Christians but we continue to demand people follow it, we are adding a burden and an unjustified condition for one's salvation. In fact, you could say we are advocating *"salvation by works."*

Significant portions of the New Testament deal with this matter, so obedience to the Mosaic Law is clearly not a trivial issue. Both Jesus and Paul were emphatic on the proper place and application of the Law for believers in Christ. Christians must know where they stand and what God expects of them, and their teachers need to preach the truth irrespective of their denominational affiliation. We should not just assume people know whether to obey the Ten Commandments or not. The message we proclaim must be clear.

Obviously, the dilemma with my Law-abiding friend forced me to study this topic further. The first and most important question I had was which position was actually correct. I looked for books that argued either for or against a Christian's obligation to obey the Law of

Moses, but I found nothing currently in print. Ones I did find just assumed the Christian's obligation to obey them. So I searched the internet only to find very short discourses on the topic or some denominational creed that provided little basis for their position. I did find some 19th century writings on the topic, but they were clearly not written for the common layman.

Writing any theological book borders on arrogance, and I hope the reader does not conclude that I think I have all the answers. But what I have learned thus far, I decided to share with you, the reader. My other hope is that this study will be simple and easy to understand so that it is useful for every Christian, from the newborn believer to the seasoned veteran. And rather than *"muddy the waters"* and confuse you by laying out the various views of each position, I will simply state what the Bible says and let the necessary conclusions fall where they may. Consequently, several Scriptures will be cited again and again so that we end up saying exactly what the Bible says and not what we may want it to say. And I apologize for the overlap between separate sections since one proof may be the premise of one and yet the conclusion of another.

Those who are unfamiliar with my previous work should know up front that I reason from two underlying premises. These must be agreed upon for any study of God's word to be fruitful. The premises are that "God is not a God of confusion,"[1] and that "the sum of Your word is truth."[2] The first premise means that God doesn't say different things in different times and places to confuse His followers. If anything, the more revelations of God we possess the better we can understand His entire word. The second premise means that God's word, when taken as a whole, is true. Parts of God's revelation cannot contradict another part. If they do (or seem to) contradict, then our understanding of one or both passages is incorrect.

It is not God or His word that causes us confusion. Rather, it is our interpretation that is misguided and wrong. So we can't just discount or altogether dismiss a verse of Scripture because it doesn't agree with our understanding or position. We must seek to understand each passage in the context in which it was written and to whom it was written to truly grasp its meaning, its application, and its purpose. Only when we approach Scripture in this way can we arrive at a better knowledge of God and His revelation.

Several denominations today clearly teach that the Ten Commandments are to be obeyed by all professing Christians. This position is typically grounded on Jesus' teaching in Matthew chapter 5. However, these denominations seem to avoid or undermine what the Apostle Paul taught. Those on the other side, who hold

---

[1] 1 Corinthians 14:33
[2] Psalm 119:160

firm to what Paul taught, seem to avoid Matthew chapter 5 or poorly explain why it doesn't say what it seems to say.

Because I believe this issue is so important, I want to be as thorough as I can and first address what defines the Law. Once we understand the Law from the position of a first century Jew, we can then show in what ways the Law was successful and in what ways it failed. This will naturally lead to why a New Covenant was promised and to whom this applies. It is my prayer that when all of this is taken into consideration, the reader will arrive at a firm, biblical understanding and application of the Mosaic Law, especially the Ten Commandments. With no more delay, let us begin.

What was the Law?

Before any fruitful discussion can begin, it is vital that we define our terms as to what is the exact meaning of the words that we are to examine. Both sides must have an agreed upon definition of what the "law" really means when we use the term "law" in the biblical sense. If what you consider to be the "law" and what I consider it to be are different, we may never arrive at a consensus merely because we have variant views of the term "law." Thus, the term "law" as it is used in the Bible (when referring to the Mosaic Law) must be adequately and clearly defined, understood, and agreed upon.

Rather than creating or forcing a preconceived definition of the "law," I believe it more scriptural and honest to let Jesus define the "law" for us. When referring to the Old Testament, Jesus either called it "the law of Moses and the Prophets and Psalms,"[3] "the law and the prophets,"[4] or simply the "law."[5] His Apostles and the other N.T. writers also used this same phraseology,[6] although at times the entire Old Testament is simply referred to as "the Scriptures."[7] So we see that the "law" was either a) solely those commandments given through Moses, b) a

---

[3] Luke 24:44
[4] Matthew 5:17-18, 7:12, 11:13, 12:5, 22:40, 23:23; Luke 10:26, 16:16-17; John 7:19-23, 8:17
[5] John 10:34
[6] Acts 13:15, 21:20, 24, 24:14, 26:22, 28:23
[7] Acts 18:24, 28

larger portion of the Old Testament including Moses' commands or c) the entire Old Testament canon.

Neither Jesus nor the apostles ever made a further delineation of the Old Testament. No writer of the New Testament broke the Old Testament into separate categories that we have accepted today. The terms *Pentateuch*, *Major* and *Minor* Prophets, *Historical* or whatever other categories our biblical predecessors have created would be completely foreign to Jesus, His apostles and the first century Jew. When a New Testament writer referred to the Mosaic "law" he meant the entire, whole, complete Law of Moses.

We should never assume that Jesus, Paul, Peter or James referred to just a section of the Law unless they were specifically quoting a passage, nor should we think that the "law" means just the Ten Commandments or even merely those commandments outside these Ten. There is nothing in all our New Testament that leads one to believe that the Ten Commandments were special or more important than the rest of the Mosaic Law. This idea is a modern import.

Similarly, neither Jesus nor His inspired apostles ever divided the Mosaic Law into *moral*, *ceremonial*, *sacrificial* or *judicial* sections. These divisions were unknown to Jesus and the Apostles as they were later scholarly divisions. If we attempt to force this later man-made delineation of the "law" upon the New Testament

11

term, we will not fully comprehend the New Testament speaker's meaning or the vastness of its application. And if we arbitrarily decide that the "law" in a certain New Testament passage does not mean all of the Mosaic "law" then we have artificially created an unbiblical definition and robbed the word of its original, intended meaning.

So when we see the term "law" in the New Testament we must and will interpret the "law" as the New Testament did. If the context is clearly referring to the Mosaic Law (and not the law of the heathen or the law of the flesh), then the word "law" means the entire Mosaic Law. It never means just the Ten Commandments or just the *sacrificial* or *ceremonial* parts of the Law. The Mosaic "law" means the whole Law delivered by Moses to the Israelites who had been redeemed from Egyptian slavery.

I hope this makes sense to you, because if you don't understand the meaning of "law" as used in the New Testament then you can become very confused. If you interpret the "law" with a definition that Jesus, Paul, or any other New Testament writer never intended you will completely misunderstand the original meaning and the impact of their statements. Once we can wrap our minds around the biblical definition of "law," we can also grasp how impactful their statements about the Mosaic Law were at the time they were written.

This realization should also bring to light how neither Jesus nor the Apostles considered the Ten

Commandments as the most important or all-encompassing part of the Mosaic Law. There is never a New Testament appeal to set apart solely the Ten Commandments. To Jesus and the Apostles, the Ten Commandments were just a part of the covenant God made with the Israelites on Mt Sinai. These first Ten were never regarded as the complete Law.

In fact, read past the Ten Commandments and you will find a plethora of additional commandments. It wasn't until after Moses had delivered these extra mandates that he asked whether the Israelites agreed to the terms of the covenant. They had a choice at this point to either agree to the terms of the covenant or to reject it in its entirety. However, they replied, "All the words which Jehovah has spoken we will do."[8] Moses then wrote down every one of the commands from chapter 20 through 23 and sprinkled the blood on the people as evidence that they had agreed to the covenant.[9]

But that's not all. Don't forget. There are also three more books: Leviticus, Numbers and Deuteronomy, which possess more commandments of this law. At the end of Leviticus it reads, "These are the commandments which Jehovah commanded Moses on Mount Sinai for the children of Israel."[10] The Jew, then, never thought that only a small section of the Law was mandatory, that

---

[8] Exodus 24:3
[9] Exodus 24:7-8
[10] Leviticus 27:34

only the Ten Commandments had to be obeyed, that only a few commands constituted the whole law. To any faithful Jew, and to Jesus as well, all of God's commandments were of equal obligation. There was never the thought that *"If I keep the first Ten, I'm good. I don't need to worry about anything else."*

God, through Moses, demanded complete obedience to the entire Law. He never gave the option to obey just some of the Law and ignore the rest. Repeatedly, the Israelite is told...

"You shall observe all My statutes and all My ordinances, and do them; I am Jehovah."[11]

"You shall not add to the word which I am commanding you, nor shall you take away from it, that you may keep the commandments of Jehovah your God."[12]

"You shall walk in all the way that Jehovah your God has commanded you."[13]

"And Jehovah commanded us to do all these statutes so that we would fear Jehovah our God."[14]

"Therefore be certain to do all the statutes and judgments that I am setting before you today"[15]

---

[11] Leviticus 19:37

[12] Deuteronomy 4:2

[13] Deuteronomy 5:33

[14] Deuteronomy 6:24

[15] Deuteronomy 11:32

"If you are not certain to do <u>all</u> the words of this law written in this book...Jehovah will raise [sickness and plague] upon you until you are destroyed"[16]
"Be certain to do <u>all</u> the works of this Law."[17]

There are many other passages that reinforce this same truth, that if you agree to the Mosaic covenant, you must obey all its requirements. A covenant, by definition, means that if one part of its conditions is not met then the entire agreement, with all its promised benefits, is void. This is why the Scriptures say, "whoever keeps the whole law yet stumbles in one point has become guilty of all,"[18] and also that "every man who becomes circumcised...he is a debtor to do the whole law."[19]

The same is true of any legal system. As a resident of a country, you are bound to obey all the laws of the land. You cannot agree to abide by a nation's civil laws and then reject its criminal laws. You cannot say, *"I pledge to not murder, but I'm not going to pay any taxes."* All laws are of equal obligation. The agreement between a government and its governed is comprehensive and all-encompassing. And it is no different with the Law of Moses.

---

[16] Deuteronomy 28:58-61
[17] Deuteronomy 31:12
[18] James 2:10
[19] Galatians 5:3

Just like the Israelite standing at the base of Mount Sinai, we, too, must choose to be bound by the entire Law or to reject it in its entirety. If we desire to obey the Law, we must commit to obey all of it. We do not have the latitude to apply the statutes we feel are important and reject those we consider irrelevant. The Law is not some smorgasbord where we pick out what we like and leave the rest.

Bearing this in mind, we should realize that if we instruct Christians (or anyone, for that matter) to obey the Ten Commandments we are, by necessary consequence, binding upon them the entire Law of Moses. The commands of Moses are not merely life principles that are good to live by. They're not nice suggestions. They are obligatory requirements of a covenant with God. We cannot divide up a covenant into necessary and optional commands, between relevant and obsolete. To be consistent, if you want to bind one part of a covenant on someone you must of necessity bind them to all of it.

Many in Christian circles today will assert that when Jesus said, "Until heaven and earth pass away, one iota or one serif shall by no means pass away from the law"[20] He meant that we today should obey the Mosaic Law. However, these same scholars conveniently redefine what Jesus meant by "the law" and assert that He meant just the Ten Commandments. For whatever reason, they

---

[20] Matthew 5:18

16

reject the biblical definition of the "law" so they can hold on to the Ten.

Perhaps they realize the complete lunacy of demanding Christians bring a yearly sacrifice to Jerusalem, that all their males be circumcised on the eighth day, that they abstain from certain foods, or even make women suspect of adultery drink bitter water.[21]   These teachers cause mass confusion since they do not obey what they confidently assert.   For if Jesus meant that Christians are to obey the Law, then Christians are bound to obey all of it, every iota and every serif.   The scope of Jesus' statement is very clear.   He referred to all the Law, not just a portion, not just the "moral" mandates, and definitely not just the Ten Commandments.

This may start to irritate some of you who highly esteem the Ten Commandments, but keep in mind that Jesus Himself did not regard the Ten Commandments as the greatest of all the commandments anyway.   Rather, He considered to "love the Lord your God with all your heart and with all your soul and with all your might,"[22] and to "love your neighbor as yourself"[23] as the most exalted. Christ said, "On these two commandments hang all the Law and the Prophets,"[24] and "There is no other

---

[21] Numbers 5:11-31
[22] Matthew 22:37, Deuteronomy 6:5
[23] Matthew 22:39, Leviticus 19:18
[24] Matthew 22:40

commandment greater than these."[25]   Every other commandment, including the Ten of Exodus 20 is merely secondary to, a fleshing out of, these two great commandments. These two undergirding commands are the origin of every Mosaic mandate.

The commands to love God and love others are greater than the Ten Commandments because they dive to the heart of the subject. One can easily resist murdering someone or sleeping with another's wife or bowing down to an idol. It is a far greater feat to not store up hatred in our hearts, or lust after another woman, or serve the gods of greed, power and self-centeredness. The Law, written on tablets of stone, can never pierce through an adamant heart.

Just like the New Testament writers, we must consider the Law as a whole, comprehensive legal system, a non-negotiable covenant. Every part of it is equally important and binding. We cannot subjectively pick and choose which commandments we feel are the most important. It's an all-or-nothing proposition. When we see the word "Law" in the New Testament, we must understand "Law" as they understood it. Whether we like it or not, whatever is said about the Law applies to every part of it, even those parts we most treasure.

---

[25] Mark 12:31

Who was to Obey the Law?

Whenever you read a book or letter it's of the utmost importance to know the context. In other words: *When* was it written, *Who* wrote it, to *Whom* was it written and *Why* was it written. You see this evident throughout the New Testament epistles. Regardless if it was Paul, Peter or even Luke, these authors made sure that each letter began with a brief mention of the author and to whom it was written. We know through historical records approximately when these letters were written, so we know who, when, and to whom it was written. Sometimes an author will tell you exactly why a letter was written[26], but most of the time you have to deduce the author's intent from the letter's contents.

The same is true with the Old Testament and, more specifically, the Law given through Moses. The first five books of the Old Testament were written for the Hebrews, the Israelites that were redeemed from Egyptian slavery. Genesis was a brief account to explain where they came from and how they fit within the scope of history. The remaining four books contain Israel's history from the birth of Moses to his death with considerable sections devoted to the covenant their God made with them.

---

[26] 1 John 5:13

The same God who created mankind was the Jehovah (YHWH) God who delivered them from slavery. This God had promised their forefather, Abraham, that He would give his descendants an inheritance of land "flowing with milk and honey."[27] Following their complete deliverance from Egyptian rule, this Jehovah (YHWH) led them to Mt. Sinai to propose an agreement, a covenant between them and him.

It is with this nation of people that God enacts the covenant we call the Mosaic Law. It is an agreement between them and their children.[28] This covenant never applied to the other nations at that time, neither to the Egyptians, the Philistines, the Amorites, the Hittites, the Armenians, the Greeks, or any other people not physically descended through Jacob (Israel). More than likely, this includes you, a Gentile.

In fact, this covenant didn't even apply to Abraham, Isaac or Jacob. This was a brand new agreement that God made with that generation of Jews. Moses said, "Not with our fathers did Jehovah make this covenant, but with us, we who are all here alive today."[29] It would be as illogical to bind this covenant upon Abraham who was not there as it would be to bind it upon Adam, Enoch, Noah or any of the other patriarchs. If you were not an Israelite present at Mt. Sinai, nor one of their physical

---

[27] Exodus 3:8

[28] Exodus 31:13, 16; Leviticus 24:8; Numbers 18:19

[29] Deuteronomy 5:3

descendants, the Law given by Moses never applied to you in the first place. In fact, it never applied to you, your father, your father's father, or your father's father's father.

Now, I know this is difficult for some people to swallow, that the Old Testament laws do not apply to them. We regard the Bible, especially the Old Testament, as the inspired word of God. It is Scripture, but simply because God's word is true and divine does not mean each instruction or commandment applies to everyone. For example, God commanded Noah to build an ark but that doesn't mean we should all become sailors. God, through Elisha, commanded Naaman to dip in the Jordan five times, but that doesn't mean we need to take 5 showers a day. When reading any work (including the Bible), it's important to know to whom it was written, and the Old Testament was written for the Israelites.

Now, we all know that when a man and woman enter into marriage the terms of that agreement are solely between that man and that woman. They are bound to one another with God as their witness. The marriage covenant is between those two persons and does not bind anyone else to that agreement. It would completely ludicrous to demand that some other woman uphold the terms of marriage with a man to whom she never married. It is as equally silly to demand other peoples obey a law given and agreed to by the Jews. We cannot substitute parties of a covenant. We cannot demand Gentiles obey a law they were never obligated to obey.

This idea should not be a surprise. The Gentiles were always outside the Law. They were "alienated from the commonwealth of Israel, and strangers to the covenants of the promise, having no hope and without God in the world."[30] Paul was perfectly clear that the Israelites alone possessed " the sonship and the glory and the covenants and the giving of the law and the service and the promises; Whose are the fathers, and out of whom, as regards what is according to flesh, is the Christ, who is God over all, blessed forever. Amen."[31]

The debate that Gentile Christians should obey the Mosaic Law was settled over 2000 years ago. As Christianity spread from Jerusalem after the stoning of Stephen, more and more Gentiles believed into Christ. So many, in fact, that these outsiders slowly became the majority within many Christian circles. The first believers in Christ were Jews, and although they still kept the Mosaic Law, they noticed these new converts did not. Eventually, Christian Jews with apparent influence started to demand these Gentile converts be circumcised and obey the Mosaic Law.

Now to us, circumcision doesn't seem that important, but to a covenant Jew it was what separated God's chosen

---

[30] Ephesians 2:12
[31] Romans 9:4-5

people from the rest of the world. Circumcision meant you were in covenant with God. Males who were not circumcised on the eighth day were cast out of the covenant and had no portion in God's promises "for the uncircumcised male who is not circumcised in the flesh of his foreskin, that person shall be cut off from his people; he has broken my covenant."[32] So before we condemn these Jews who were zealous for God's law, it may be they had an honest concern that these new converts might be jeopardizing their salvation.

The teaching of these Judaizers was "unless you [Gentiles] are circumcised according to the custom of Moses, you cannot be saved."[33] Paul and Barnabas, had just finished their first missionary journey throughout the Roman Empire and consequently converted many Gentiles, and they clearly never taught that non-Jews needed to be circumcised to be saved. Thus, there arose a huge "dissension" among the church.[34]

Apparent that no resolution or compromise was in sight, it was decided by the church to send representatives from both sides to the Apostles and elders in Jerusalem to decide the matter. When these arrived and shared how many Gentiles had believed into Christ, more Jewish Christians showed up and demanded that "It is necessary

---

[32] Genesis 17:14
[33] Acts 15:1
[34] Acts 15:2

to circumcise them and to charge them to keep the law of Moses."[35]

Notice how similar the Judaizers' message is to what we hear today from many pulpits: *"You must obey the Old Testament and especially the Ten Commandments. You need to take one day off of work each week to honor the Sabbath. You must tithe all of your income to the church."* However, churches today aren't commanding that all their males be circumcised. We aren't verifying that all our men have had their foreskin removed? But if the covenant made between the Israelites and God is binding upon a Gentile, then why isn't the covenant made between Abraham and God also binding? At least the first century Judaizers were consistent.

But what is most conclusive from the Jerusalem council is the final verdict of the Apostles and elders. Now, keep in mind that every one of the leaders of the church at this point was a Jew. The Gentiles had no vote or sway over this forthcoming decision. And undoubtedly, Peter knew Jesus' statement from Matthew 5 because Peter was there. He saw and heard everything Jesus said and did since the day of His baptism until He was taken up into Heaven.[36] In addition, Christ promised Peter, one of the twelve chosen apostles, that the Holy Spirit would "guide you

---

[35] Acts 15:5
[36] Acts 1:21-22

into all the reality [truth]."[37] So when Peter spoke, people listened, because they knew he "had been with Jesus."[38]

This same Peter, who was specifically chosen to reach the Jews,[39] "rose up and said to the entire assembly, "God, the Knower of hearts, bore witness to them [Gentiles], giving them the Holy Spirit even as also to us [Jews]; And He made no distinction between us and them, cleansing their hearts by faith...But we believe that through the grace of the Lord Jesus we are saved in the same way also as they are."[40] The Apostle Peter knew and clearly stated that all believers, Jew or Gentile, had their hearts cleansed and were saved by faith. Faith was the sole effectual means by which a sinner received salvation. Peter made no mention of following any part of the Mosaic Law, even the Ten Commandments. In fact, Peter's statements completely contradicted the Judaizers' claim.

Peter undoubtedly remembered what God taught him during and following his vision on the roof of the tanner's home.[41] Peter went into the home of the uncircumcised and preached the good news of Jesus Christ. Cornelius, without any prior obedience to the Law, was baptized by

---

[37] John 16:13
[38] Acts 4:13
[39] Galatians 2:8
[40] Acts 15:9,11
[41] Acts 10:15

25

the Holy Spirit and was baptized into Christ.[42] God gave these Gentiles his stamp of approval because of their faith in the good news of Jesus Christ. For this point forward, there was no longer clean and unclean, Jew and Gentile, but only those in Christ and those not of His body.

Having experienced the life-altering change that God's grace brings, Peter had grown to recognize the Mosaic Law as a "yoke...which neither our fathers nor we were able to bear."[43] He didn't think the Law was some good rule to live by. He, being born under the Law, experientially knew and believed the exact opposite, that the Law was a burdensome yoke. Peter viewed the charge that Gentiles should obey the Law as an affront to God. He accused these Judaizers who would bind the Law upon believers as "testing God."[44] It was evident to Peter, who again knew Matthew 5:17-20, that God had already made His decision when He sent His Spirit upon those who had received Christ through faith.

The argument against obedience to the Law gets even stronger when James, the leading bishop of the Jerusalem church, declared that Gentile believers were solely to "1) abstain from things that have been sacrificed to idols and 2) blood and 3) things strangled and 4) fornication."[45] These were the only burdens that all the Apostles with

---

[42] Acts 10:44-46
[43] Acts 15:10b
[44] Acts 15:10a
[45] Acts 15:29

"one accord"[46] sought to enforce upon Gentile Christians. There is no mention of the Ten Commandments, of circumcision, of keeping the Sabbath or even tithing.

It is certainly clear from the council in Jerusalem and throughout Paul's letters that no Gentile was ever commanded to obey the Mosaic Law. What so many of us have done is confuse the obligation of an Old Covenant Jew with that of a New Covenant Christian. The interpretation that Matthew 5 means that the old Law is still valid and should be obeyed is contradicted historically by the first hand witnesses of Christ's words. If Jesus really meant that Christians should obey the Law, then the Apostles who were chosen by Christ to relay His message would have taught such. However, the Apostles and the early church preached the very opposite and never mandated an obedience to the Mosaic Law.

Anyone who differs with Peter or Paul must explain how they know better than Christ's chosen apostles. Those who disagree, who teach that Gentile Christians should obey the Law, must convince us how they are more led by the Spirit, how they better understand the very Scriptures that the Apostles themselves wrote. The preponderance of evidence throughout the New Testament agrees with the decision of the Jerusalem council, that "a man is not justified out of works of law"[47] and "out of the works of the law no flesh shall be justified

---

[46] Acts 15:25
[47] Galatians 2:16

before Him."[48] Those who teach otherwise have their one passage in Matthew 5 that they fail to understand (but more about this later).

Why was the Law Replaced?

Many of us have grown up with a critical parent or been affected by a negative spouse, friend or relative. No matter what you do it is never good enough. If you failed at something, you knew they would point it out. You knew you'd hear about it. *"I told you so!"* *"You'll never make it!"* *"You just can't do anything right!"* We consequently learned how to fake perfection, hide our failures, mask our faults, numb the pain, or we just stopped trying altogether. We knew we'd never live up to their idea of perfection. We'd never gain their approval.

The patriarch Jacob knew how this felt all too well. His father favored his brother. He had to trade for his brother's birthright and steal his brother's blessing just to hear a compliment from his dad. In fear of his brother's rage, he moved and acquired in-laws who only manipulated and used him. His father-in-law accused him of theft, and his wives just blamed him. Fleeing these in-laws, Jacob was officially worn out, frustrated, and exasperated.

It's no surprise, then, why Jacob wrestled with God's angel throughout the night. All the disappointment, all the frustration of never being good enough was at a head. This "man" wasn't going anywhere until he had gained His approval. Someone was going to accept him.

Someone had to love him just the way he was as he said, "I will not let You go unless You bless me."[49]

This yearning for acceptance, this absence of approval could only be quenched by Almighty God. His dad didn't do it. His wives couldn't do it. Only God could offer complete forgiveness and acceptance. It was this final ditch effort that led God to forever change Jacob's name to "Israel, for you have struggled with God and with men and have prevailed."[50] The name by which all of the Hebrews, all of his descendants would be known from that day forward was the Israelites. They would forever be defined as a nation that struggled with God and men. Jacob, their forefather, had finally received the Father's blessing. The hope of every true Israelite.

We, Christians, have the same hope of God's approval, but ours is guaranteed for "He graced us in the Beloved."[51] However, those under the Law did not have this guarantee. Their acceptance and approval was based upon works, on how well they followed the Law. We, living under a system of grace, have grown up with a romantic view of the Mosaic Law, but this is because we have never had to live under it. We don't truly know what it's like to live under a system of works, that everything you do will *"make or break you,"* that you

---

[49] Genesis 32:26
[50] Genesis 32:28
[51] Ephesians 1:6

have to earn God's approval, that you have to *"pull yourself up by your own bootstraps."*

In this way, the Mosaic Law was no different than the hundreds of other religious views at the time. You did your best and offered sacrifices to appease the gods with the hope they would not rain their wrath upon you. The Mosaic Law was a system that only condemned and never guaranteed the complete blessing and acceptance of God. It relied upon one's perfect obedience. There was no present Savior, no "Lamb of God who takes away the sin of the world." [52] It was only foreknown through faith in God's promises.

Today, we, Christians, like to take vacations in the Law, but we always return to our home of grace. Similarly, we can join a church sponsored missionary journey to help those suffering under an oppressive government. We can *"feel their pain"* and try to offer hope, but the difference is: we get to fly home. We may feel genuine sympathy for those downtrodden, those neglected and abused by an oppressive system, but we truly don't know what it feels like to be without any real hope of freedom.

The Jew, however, knew exactly how it felt to live under a rigid system of law keeping, under a regime that demanded perfect obedience or a swift, deadly recompense or delayed damnation. Imagine the guilt every time you brought one of your own lambs to be

---

[52] John 1:29

slaughtered because of your transgressions. You messed up and now an innocent animal had to suffer and be killed. If we had to murder one of our pets every time we sinned, imagine how few pets would be in our homes.

God demanded the Israelites offer a daily morning and evening sacrifice in addition to all the new month, new moon, and other feasts.[53] Each and every day the Jews endured the smell of burnt flesh permeated the city as a constant reminder of their people's sin. We think we understand the Law, but we don't. We can't adequately imagine what it was like. We can't know the feeling of despair, always worried about the coming wrath of God, just hoping we've done enough. Paul, however, knew exactly how living under the Law felt.

---

[53] See Numbers 28:1-29:40

The Law cannot Free!

We know the Apostle Paul as the great evangelist of the Roman Empire, but before he became a Christian missionary he was a terrorist on a mission to destroy the church. He was "a Pharisee, a son of Pharisees"[54] who excelled all his contemporaries in Judaism.[55] He zealously defended not only the Mosaic Law but the traditions of his fathers. He broke into homes and threw Christians in prison to testify at their death.[56] He was the least likely candidate to ever become a Christian, yet his life experience under the Law made him the greatest advocate for God's grace.

One would suppose that Paul would have retained an esteemed view of the Law like so many today attempt to convince the world of its awesomeness. But, rather, Paul writes time and time again about the inadequacy of the Law, how it failed to save anyone, and how it was ultimately a curse to man. He says, "As many as are of the works of law are under a curse; for it is written, Cursed is everyone who does not continue in all the things written in the book of the law to do them."[57] It wasn't as if the Law just failed to save its subjects, but it imprisoned them under a curse.

---

[54] Acts 23:6
[55] Galatians 1:14
[56] Acts 26:10
[57] Deuteronomy 27:26; Galatians 3:10

The Israelites, and Paul included, lived under a curse of perfection to "be holy, for I am holy."[58] They lived in a constant state of fear knowing that "he who does them shall live because of them."[59] In other words, they survived by keeping every commandment, every statute, and every ordinance. Any slip, any mistake, meant death (either immediately or ultimately). There was no grace, no mercy, and no leniency. It was very simple: Keep the Law perfectly. Any person living under this system was constantly aware of their failure to reach the glory of God.

And yet, no matter how perfect you did keep the commandments you could never be truly sinless. You could never be fully righteous. That's why Christ could say, "Unless your righteousness surpasses that of the scribes and Pharisees you shall by no means enter into the kingdom of the heavens."[60] The Pharisees did keep the literal commandments of the Law perfectly, but even this perfect adherence to the Law could not make them righteous before God. Imagine the shock this statement had on the average Jew who heard this: that the most religious, most zealous teachers of the Law were not righteous, that even they would not inherit the Kingdom. If they couldn't, then who could?

---

[58] Leviticus 11:44
[59] Jeremiah 18:5; Galatians 3:12
[60] Matthew 5:20

The honest realization of falling short carries with it a degree of guilt, knowing that one is not sinless, one is not righteous before a holy God. The repeated and continuous offering of sacrifices just increased the realization that the Law was "unable to perfect, according to conscience, him who worships."[61] The offender may have left the altar being declared *"forgiven"* by the priest, but the guilt remained. The Jew was never free from his poor lack of performance, and the constant airing of his failures to obtain forgiveness only solidified his guilt and shame.

This is because the Law was never instituted to free man from sin. Rather, it was instituted to increase transgression, to raise our awareness of our exceeding sinfulness, "that it might be shown to be sin by working out death in me through that which is good [the Law], that sin through the commandment [of the Law] might become exceedingly sinful."[62] The Law never freed anyone from sin. Rather, it did the opposite. It became a tool of sin by "seizing the opportunity through the commandment [of the Law], deceived me and through it killed me."[63]

The Law never has and never will free us from the power and dominion of sin and death because "the power of sin

---

[61] Hebrews 9:9
[62] Romans 7:13
[63] Romans 7:11

is the law."[64] From the time of Adam "sin entered into the world, and through sin, death."[65] And up until this very day every unregenerate person still dwells in and is a slave to sin as David said, "in sin did my mother conceive me."[66] Sin, even through the Law, has conquered man and made him a slave. There was never a chance that one could obtain one's own freedom through the Law. Someone else, the Lamb of God, had to become a curse in our stead and pay the ransom price for our freedom.

The idea of a ransom payment was well understood during the time of the New Testament's writing. A ransom was a price paid to free a slave or a prisoner of war. There was no other way by which a slave or a prisoner of war could obtain his freedom. The slave could not proffer any item of value to pay off his master since his master already owned it. The captive of war could not use his possessions to pay for his release since the victor now owned them. Someone else had to provide the full payment. The slave or the prisoner of war had no way to obtain their freedom on their own.

Just as the slave or the captive could never make the payment for their freedom, the Law could never meet the price set for our release. The Law, in effect, only increased the cost of our freedom, a cost that demanded the death of the offender. Just as with a credit account,

---

[64] 1 Corinthians 15:56
[65] Romans 5:12
[66] Psalms 51:5

each of our infractions only increase the outstanding balance, and the Law only adds more and more debits to our account. The Mosaic Law, in the end, only condemned man.

And this condemnation through "the law works out wrath."[67] As we tally up our failures, our transgressions, our mishaps, we only fall even further under God's righteous wrath. Just like the Gentiles, the Jews "also all conducted ourselves once in the lusts of our flesh, doing the desires of the flesh and of the thoughts, and were by nature children of wrath, even as the rest."[68] The Law's legal decrees never demonstrated our holiness but, rather, amplified our sinfulness, our utter failure to reach perfection. The Law left everyone subject to the holy wrath of God.

God, being righteous and holy, cannot tolerate sin. He cannot accept it in His presence or condone it throughout His creation. To tolerate it, to turn a blind eye to sin, would be to ignore justice. Our God would be no good god at all if he failed to bring judgment against the liar, against the thief, against the adulterer, against the sexually perverse, against the murderer, or rapist or child molester.

A God who just ignores sin is no different than a parent who allows his children to hurt one another or a

---

[67] Romans 4:15
[68] Ephesians 2:1-3

government that allows injustice. When evil occurs, when people are killed, when women are raped, when children are taken as sex slaves, people cry out and demand justice against the perpetrator. And likewise all of creation, the seen and the unseen, the rulers and principalities in the heavens, demand justice against man because of his sins. The Law only cements this condemnation "that the offense might abound"[69] for it amplifies man's gross failure.

This is why Paul, a master of the Law, could call the Law a "ministry of death."[70] Its presence and purpose was only to increase transgression, but never to rectify it. Yes, the Law, in and of itself, is "holy."[71] Its commands are true and right, but it was instituted to grant a "clear knowledge of sin,"[72] to make us realize how much we needed a Savior. The Law was given that sin might be shown to be "exceedingly sinful"[73] so "that every mouth may be stopped and all the world may fall under the judgment of God."[74]

Without God's saving grace, without the atonement of Christ's death, if all you had was the Law, you would be

---

[69] Romans 5:20
[70] 2 Corinthians 3:7
[71] Romans 7:12
[72] Romans 3:20
[73] Romans 7:13
[74] Romans 3:19

"dead in your offenses and sins"[75] Everyone, Jew and Gentile, is destined for the righteous judgment of God, and without the redemption that is through the cross we all are damned to eternal destruction. Whether born a Jew or a Gentile, we are all "children of wrath."[76] It makes no difference for "both Jews and Greeks...are all under sin. Even as it is written, "There is none righteous, not even one."[77] "For as many as have sinned without the law shall also perish without the law; and as many as have sinned under the law shall be judged by the law."[78]

---

[75] Ephesians 2:1
[76] Ephesians 2:3
[77] Romans 3:10
[78] Romans 2:12

The Law cannot Justify!

During my years working with God's people, I've met many faithful, repentant believers in various denominations of the Lord's body. One characteristic that was common to them all was a bankruptcy of spirit.[79] Each one was cognizant of their own spiritual failure thereby creating a longing and thirst for God's righteousness. Each was inherently concerned with their relationship and standing with God. Every one of them possessed a reverence for God's revealed word. I imagine that much of one's admiration for the Mosaic Law is due to this type of godly character. I highly doubt that most Christians who esteem the Law do so in order to glorify themselves or judge others.

However, we must remember that the Mosaic Law, including the Ten Commandments, was replaced with a new and far better covenant[80] for a reason. It wasn't as if God thought the Law was sufficient. It wasn't as if God was unprepared if man chose to reject His authority. Our Father had already planned before the foundation of the world to choose, call and justify people through faith in His Son.[81] The Law was a temporary bridge, a "child-conductor" leading us to Christ.[82] It was "weak through

---

[79] Matthew 5:3

[80] Jeremiah 31:31-34; Hebrews 8:13

[81] See Ephesians 1:1-14

[82] Galatians 3:25, 4:3

the flesh"[83] and unable to justify even the most obedient and faithful believer.

Justification is a legal term. It does not mean *"just as if I never sinned."* Justification means to be declared righteous in a courtroom. For example, God commanded, "If there is a dispute between men, and they approach the court, and the judges judge them, they shall justify the righteous and condemn the wicked."[84] Some modern translations replace the word "justify" with *"to be made right with God,"* but this is not the meaning by which the Scriptures use this term.

When we view the usage of justification in the New Testament, there are only two meanings attributed to it. The foremost definition follows the Jewish understanding of a declaration of righteousness in court. The second use of the term is seen in Luke when Jesus declares, "wisdom is justified by all her children."[85] It's not as if wisdom is standing in God's courtroom to be declared righteous, but, rather, wisdom is vindicated by her offspring. This is also how James used the term "justification." He writes, "You see that a man is justified by works and not by faith only."[86]

---

[83] Romans 8:3
[84] Deuteronomy 25:1
[85] Luke 7:35
[86] James 2:24

Now James' statement confuses many people who believe it to contradict Paul who wrote, "man is not justified out of works of law, but through faith in Jesus Christ."[87] But if we know that justification can have two meanings, the apparent contradiction disappears and again, the sum of God's word is true. But, bear in mind, unless the context demands that we understand justification as vindication, we must utilize its primary and default definition which is the declaration of one's righteousness in a legal setting.

Now, if a person solely offers as evidence his or her obedience to the Law, his or her good works, that person will still be found guilty. You could show how you obeyed, not only the Ten Commandments but, the entire Mosaic Law perfectly and guess what? You're still guilty. A person's good deeds can never declare one righteous before God. As the prophet Isaiah said, "all our righteousnesses are like a soiled garment."[88] This doesn't mean our works are not good in themselves, just as it doesn't mean our disobedience renders God's laws unrighteous. It simply means that if we threw all our good works in a basket and offered it to God as the basis of our righteousness we would still be found lacking.

Faith, repentance, confession, baptism and good works mean nothing without the finished work of Jesus Christ. No matter how good we are, how perfect we follow God's laws, if Christ had not died for our sins we could

---

[87] Galatians 2:16

[88] Isaiah 64:6

never be saved. We could never be justified before God. Our faith and our faithful obedience to God are both meaningless if Christ had not died. God could not nor would not declare any one of us as righteous without the blood payment of Christ.

The entire argument that one could be justified before God through works, even works of the Law, negates the very reason Christ died. For "if righteousness is through law, then Christ died for nothing."[89] Think about it. If you could just obey the Law, "*be a good person*" and be accounted righteous on the Day of Judgment, then why did Christ come and die in the first place? Why didn't He just come and tell us to obey the Law and be "*good*" people? The answer is simple: you cannot be declared righteous before God through the Law or through all your "*goodness*."

That is the reason so many reject the gospel of Jesus Christ. They believe "the lie"[90] that they are "*good enough*," that they cannot be judged by anyone, even by a God whom they do not recognize. The reality that they could not be declared righteous before the Creator is ludicrous to them. The world cannot stomach the idea that "there is salvation in no other, for neither is there another name under heaven given among men in which we must be saved."[91]

---

[89] Galatians 2:21
[90] Romans 1:25
[91] Acts 4:12

The world likes to think everyone is good at heart and whatever god does exist should accept everyone. The world, and even some churches, think God will accept people just as they are: without faith, without repentance, without Christ's blood stained on their wedding garments. I've even heard some believers angrily accuse God at the thought that He would not justify people due to their unbelief or repentance from dead works. To all of them, Christ is "foolishness and a stone of stumbling."[92]

This same train of thought was evident when Eve reasoned that God was her equal. She believed she had the right to do whatever she wanted, that she could be her own god and should be accepted just as she was. We are no different when we assert that God must accept us, or our precious grandma, because of all the good things we or they have done, because we are *"good people,"* because we aren't nearly as bad as the *"other"* people?

We sadly like to make mental lists of how *"good"* we are, how we never lie, never cheat, never curse, how we obey the Ten Commandments and honor the Sabbath, how we don't drink alcohol, don't party, don't commit adultery, and especially aren't one of those homosexuals. We consequently feel justified in ourselves. This, my friends, is what we call self-righteousness, judging ourselves by the standard of ourselves. It is a righteousness based upon our own merit, upon how good

[92] Romans 9:32

we are, upon what we did or didn't do, upon who are versus who we aren't. It is no different than the Pharisee who exclaimed, "I thank You that I am not like the rest of men...I fast twice a week; I give a tenth of all that I get."[93] Yet this law-keeping Pharisee did not go home justified, and neither do we whenever we base our justification on what we do.

We have all "been weighed in the scales and found to be lacking,"[94] and that is why the Law was given: to prove to mankind that he has fallen far from perfection. The Law not only made us aware that coveting was wrong[95] but that all sin is "exceedingly sinful"[96] so "that every mouth may be stopped and all the world may fall under the judgment of God; Because out of the works of the law no flesh shall be justified before Him; for through the law is the clear knowledge of sin."[97]

---

[93] Luke 18:11-12
[94] Daniel 5:27
[95] Romans 7:7
[96] Romans 7:13
[97] Romans 3:19-20

The Law cannot Perfect!

Every single day the Mosaic high priest offered a sacrifice for sins. Why? Because it was retroactive. It forgave the sins (or more accurately postponed the judgment of those sins) which were previously committed. It could not forgive the sin not yet committed, "For the law...can never by the same sacrifices year by year, which they offer continually, perfect those who draw near. Otherwise would they not have ceased to be offered?"[98]

If the Law could have ever perfected people, they would have just offered one big sacrifice and been done with it. But the temporary blood of goats and sheep and bulls could never make an eternal atonement "for it is impossible for the blood of bulls and goats to take away sins."[99] The animal sacrifices offered under the Law could never atone for our transgressions. Now, Scripture never tells us why but I think (and this is my opinion) that this is because the life of an animal does not equal the life of a human made in the image of God. The sacrificed life must be equal to the value of the life being redeemed. That's why Christ had to become a man to pay this ransom.

---

[98] Hebrews 10:1-2
[99] Hebrews 10:4

I know that when I lie and cheat and hurt people, I never dream that my wickedness could be rectified through the killing of an innocent bystander. I transgressed God's law, and I deserve the punishment. If my thinking is correct, I would assume that the people of old realized this: that they, themselves, were the ones who deserved to die for their own sin. Perhaps they knew this, but continued to offer their sacrifices with faith that God would finally and absolutely deal with their sin problem. They knew deep down that someone else had to make full payment for their failure and they knew that these finite animal sacrifices only pointed to the Messiah, Who would die in their stead. They understood that "if Christ has not been raised...you are still in your sins."[100] In other words, the Mosaic Law with all of its sacrifices could never forgive us our sins.

Christ commanded that we are to "be perfect as your heavenly Father is perfect."[101] To one who truly comprehends what a great feat this is, this perfection is impossible. Every honest Jew during Jesus' time knew that ""whoever keeps the whole law yet stumbles in one point has become guilty of all."[102] The Israelite knew he was guilty and guilty all the time. He knew no matter how hard he tried he still fell short of God's glory.[103]

---

[100] 1 Corinthians 15:17

[101] Matthew 5:48

[102] James 2:10

[103] It is only because our eyes are so thoroughly tainted and blinded by sin that we can so ignorantly view

This is why Peter referred to the Law as a "yoke...with neither our fathers nor we were able to bear."[104]

The yoke was used by farmers to bind an animal or animals to draw a plough or pull heavy loads. It was a wooden piece placed around the neck of the animal, to forcibly control it to do whatever the master desired. God referred to Israel's slavery in Egypt as a yoke in saying, "I have broken the bars of your yoke and made you walk upright."[105] When a Jew heard the term yoke he instantly knew what that meant, that it was used to oppress, bind, and control the subject.

The Law was a yoke that served exactly this same purpose. It bound the Jew to obey its commands or face immediate punishment. Just as an animal that refused to do what the master wanted the Law immediately corrected and chastised the person for failing to be perfect. And it never stopped. You were never free,

---

ourselves as "*good*". We cannot fathom the depravity of our sin and rebellion. We are blind to how our own wickedness destroys our souls and those around us. We call ourselves "*good*" and we have no basis to even make such a declaration. We are so mired with sin we don't even recognize how the most minute thought, self-centered deed or uncaring action makes us so far from perfect that God had to send His Son to die in our stead. How ignorant we are when we offer up to God our good works as if this somehow negates all of our self-centered wickedness.

[104] Acts 15:10
[105] Leviticus 26:13

never justified, never perfect enough. The Law was there to continually indict and punish you for every infraction. It was a never ending assault and endless burden. Those under Law were continually aware of their failure, always conscious of their sins, "otherwise would they [the sacrifices] not have ceased to be offered, because those worshipping, having once been purified, would have no longer had the consciousness of sins?"[106] But as it was, the Jew was always conscious of his sin.

The reality is the Law of Moses was and is "weak through the flesh."[107] In other words, this "ministry of death"[108] that operates through our flesh is too weak an adversary for sin. Our spirit may be willing, it may want to do what's right, but as long as we dwell in this flesh that is predisposed to rebel against God we will never always choose to do the right thing. No matter how many good rules are within the Law, it still did not, nor could not, battle the flesh effectively. The Law was a 100-pound weakling against a 500-pound gorilla called our flesh.

We should always remember that "the law is not enacted for a righteous man but for the lawless and unruly, for the ungodly and sinners, for the unholy and profane."[109] Governments don't make laws for honest people. Laws are made because someone previously abused their

---

[106] Hebrews 10:2
[107] Romans 8:3
[108] 2 Corinthians 3:7
[109] 1 Timothy 1:9

freedom. Yes, "the Law is holy, righteous and good,"[110] but its rules are elementary at best. They scratch the surface of holiness. They hint towards a better way. They point us toward perfection, but can never deliver us to that state. Just as the corruptible flesh must die to be raised incorruptible,[111] the commandments had to be set aside "because of its weakness and unprofitableness (for the law perfected nothing)."[112]

"If indeed...perfection were through the Levitical priesthood...what need was there still that a different Priest should arise according to the order of Melchizedek?"[113] If God's plan was to keep the Mosaic Law, He would have also kept the Levitical priests. But He didn't. He replaced this priesthood just as He had promised. But the new High Priest wouldn't need to offer sacrifices for His own sins because He would be sinless.[114] This different Priest wouldn't need to transfer His office to his son because He would never die.[115]

---

[110] Romans 7:12
[111] 1 Corinthians 15:53-54
[112] Hebrews 7:18
[113] Hebrews 7:11
[114] 2 Corinthians 5:21, 1 Peter 1:19
[115] Hebrews 7:24-28

50

What Replaced the Law?

A Better Covenant

Any Jew in the first century was well aware that a Prophet[116] like Moses would deliver a new covenant as it is written, "A Prophet will I raise up for them from the midst of their brothers like you. And I will put My words in His mouth, and He will speak to them all that I command Him. And the man who will not listen to My words which He will speak in My name, I Myself will require it from him."[117] Jesus was the physical seed, yet the eternal Lord of David."[118] He is the rightful King of God's people and, through His death and resurrection, Jesus fulfilled Jeremiah's prophecy,

"Indeed, days are coming, declares Jehovah, when I will make a new covenant with the house of Israel and with the house of Judah. Not like the covenant which I made with their fathers...But this is the covenant which I will make with the house of Israel...I will put My law within them and write it upon their hearts; and I will be their God, and they will be My people. And they will no longer teach, each man his neighbor and each man his brother, saying, Know Jehovah; for all of them will know Me, from the little one among them even to the great one

---

[116] John 1:21, 6:14, 7:40
[117] Deuteronomy 18:18-19
[118] Psalms 110:1

among them, declares Jehovah, for I will forgive their iniquity, and their sin I will remember no more."[119]

This new covenant was enacted following Jesus' death as He said, "this is My blood of the covenant, which is being poured out for many for forgiveness of sins."[120] When a man creates a *new will and testament* to determine what will be done with his estate following his death only the latest will has any binding authority. "For where there is a testament, the death of him who made the testament must of necessity be established...since it never has force when he who made the testament is living. Hence, neither was the first covenant initiated without blood."[121]

And since Jesus' death is well established, the old will and testament, the Mosaic Law, is completely null and void as it is written, "He takes away the first that He may establish the second."[122] The new law, Christ's law, cannot be in force until the first law is done away with. And God took away the first law when "Christ, who through the eternal Spirit offered Himself without blemish to God" and thus became, "the Mediator of a new covenant."[123]

---

[119] Jeremiah 31:31-34
[120] Matthew 26:28
[121] Hebrews 9:16-18
[122] Hebrews 10:9
[123] Hebrews 9:14-15

And "in saying, a new covenant, He has made the first old."[124] So when we speak of the old covenant, we mean the Mosaic Law and everything it comprises. And when we speak of the Mosaic Law we understand that, to God, it is old and has no binding authority. Now, don't get too upset at this proclamation for even the Scriptures say, "since the priesthood is transferred, of necessity there comes into being a transfer of law also."[125]

Undoubtedly, some will argue that God merely transferred the old Law to a different high priest but did not necessary replace the old Mosaic Law. But what does the Scripture say? "He takes away the first that He may establish the second."[126] Jesus did not magically become a Levitical priest when He became High Priest for He was "a Priest forever according to the order of Melchisedec."[127] Long before Moses, Abraham gave a tenth to his superior Melchisedec. And just as Abraham was inferior to Melchisedec, the law given through Moses is inferior to the law given by Christ.

Also, a covenant, by definition, contains its agreed upon terms. Thus, every covenant has its own unique terms. The covenant made with Noah is different than the covenant made with Abraham. In addition, a covenant cannot be agreed upon until its terms are defined. This is

---

[124] Hebrews 8:13
[125] Hebrews 7:12
[126] Hebrews 10:9
[127] Hebrews 5:6

why Moses delivered God's commandments to the Israelites before they agreed to them and why Moses did not seal the covenant with blood until after their acceptance to its terms.

So if God made a new covenant with His people and if this new covenant was initiated by His Son's blood, then this new covenant by necessity has a new law, which are the very commandments Jesus delivered. But why did God replace the Law? Because, as we've already learned, perfection was not attainable through it. Through all the Levitical laws, through all its sacrifices, the Law and its ordinances could never perfect those who followed it. That's why He replaced it. God fulfilled His promises when His Son offered His blood as the seal of the new covenant and, thus, made His new law binding upon all His disciples.

Jesus offered the perfect eternal sacrifice for sins and consequently initiated the new covenant as He said Himself, "This cup is the new covenant established in My blood, which is being poured out for you."[128] And since the new covenant has been initiated, the old Law's commands are moot. They are obsolete. The old, decrepit and "disappearing"[129] Law has no binding authority whatsoever because it has been replaced. Period.

---

[128] Luke 22:20
[129] Hebrews 8:13

Now, at this point some will concede that Gentiles are not subject to the Mosaic Law but still assert that Jews are still bound to obey it. However, if you read the passage from Jeremiah 31 again you will notice that God promised to make a new covenant with Israel and Judah, not the Gentiles. In fact, if this new covenant was put into effect then neither the Jew nor the Gentile are subject to the old Law given through Moses.

In the same vein, some will also try to argue that God has different requirements for Jewish Christians and Gentile Christians. However, if there be one new covenant, "one body and one Spirit...one Lord, one faith, one baptism; One God,"[130] then there cannot be two laws, two requirements for entry into the one kingdom of God. God has not divided His kingdom between two Lords or two avenues by which one can be saved for even Jesus said, "No one comes to the Father except through Me."[131] This fallacy leads to confusion and makes God favor a person based upon their parentage, but we know that "Everyone who believes on Him shall not be put to shame. For there is no distinction between Jew and Greek, for the same Lord is Lord of all and rich to all who call upon Him; For whoever calls upon the name of the Lord shall be saved."[132] As it is written elsewhere, "there is no respect of persons with God."[133]

---

[130] Ephesians 4:4-6
[131] John 14:6
[132] Romans 10:11-13
[133] Romans 2:11 (see also Ephesians 6:9)

I have even heard some teach that anyone who believes into Christ (a.k.a. the church) is the new Israel. They infer this from Paul when he wrote these two statements, "not all who are out of Israel are Israel; Neither is it that because they are the seed of Abraham, they are all children; but, In Isaac shall your seed be called, That is, it is not the children of the flesh who are the children of God, but the children of the promise are accounted as the seed,"[134] and, "For he is not a Jew who is one outwardly; neither is circumcision that which is outward in the flesh. But he is a Jew who is one inwardly; and circumcision is of the heart."[135]

However, this interpretation of Scripture presupposes a position that the text does not actually say. Paul never states that believing Gentiles were the true Israel. He only points out that those Israelites who "pursued [righteousness] not out of faith, but as it were out of works"[136] were not the Israel of faith. These unfaithful Israelites were merely Jews according to the flesh. Paul also never says that believing Gentiles are the real Jews because their circumcision is of the heart. Again, he only points out that the false Jew, the Israelite who broke his covenant with God, was not a genuine Jew.[137]

---

[134] Romans 9:6-8

[135] Romans 2:28-29

[136] Romans 9:32

[137] You can easily see how this is wrong when we apply simple math to Romans 9:6. If A = "All of Israel", and B = "Israel"; then,

56

In addition, if we were to accept that Paul meant that the church was the true Israel then the meaning of the terms "Jew" and "Israel" are confusing throughout Paul's epistles. Note that immediately following Paul's discourse on a "Jew who is one inwardly," he proceeds to discuss the advantages of being a Jew in chapter 3. Well, that doesn't make any sense if he is referring to the church, or Gentiles for that matter. And, later in the same letter, Paul explains that "hardness has come upon Israel in part until the fullness of the Gentiles comes in."[138] Does that mean that the church has been hardened? Obviously not. None of Paul's teachings make any sense if we confuse the terms as he, and the rest of Scripture, consistently uses them.

Yet, are all those of faith the adopted children of God? Yes. Are we then Abraham's seed? Yes. But the church, comprised of Jew and Gentile, is never called Israel. It's called a different name, the church, for a reason. This Israel re-definition is a spiritual magic wand theologians use to support a theory that is not explicitly taught in Scripture. We must remember that if a doctrine is not explicitly stated in Scripture it is mere conjecture and

---

according to Paul, Not all of A = B ("Not all of Israel are Israel"), but only some of A = B. Stated negatively, all of A≠B. There is no mention of G, the Gentile, or C, the church. Paul does not posit an equation that says: "Not all of A = B, but C = B."

[138] Romans 11:25 (see also Luke 21:24)

susceptible to man's infinite fallibility. As it stands, faithless Jews are no different than faithless Gentiles. Neither can be accounted righteousness before God without faith for "without faith it is impossible to be well pleasing to Him."[139]

Of course this argument that we, Gentiles, somehow mystically become the true Israel is actually moot in regards to our obligatory obedience to the Law. Even if one holds to this view, one cannot then claim that an Israelite is bound to obey the old Mosaic Law for we have a new high priest. We have a new covenant secured with the blood of Jesus Christ and, consequently, we have a new law. The old law has been made obsolete and even in the first century it was "near to disappearing."[140]

This is why Paul so aggressively attacked anyone who would teach Christians mandatory obedience to the Mosaic Law. He, without hesitation, called them "false brothers, brought in secretly, who stole in to spy out our freedom which we have in Christ Jesus, that they might bring us into slavery."[141] He wasn't wishy washy concerning this issue. He made it perfectly clear that "every man who becomes circumcised that he is a debtor to do the whole law" and that "you who are being justified by law, you have fallen from grace."[142] Anyone

---

[139] Hebrews 11:6
[140] Hebrews 8:13
[141] Galatians 2:4
[142] Galatians 3:3-4

who believes that by obeying even one command of the old Law he becomes more favorable to God this one has fallen from grace. This one has forfeited the only real basis of justification, Christ's death, to attempt to justify himself.

With such obvious evidence, why do we still have a difficult time letting go of the Law? Even after knowing the liberating freedom found in Christ, why do we still say under our breath "The old is better?"[143] The Jews in Rome had this same problem, so Paul used an elementary illustration to demonstrate how all Christians were dead to the Law. He likened the Christian's divorce from the Mosaic Law to a wife whose husband had died and then marries another. The Law, in this sense, was our former husband who is now dead, and we aren't any more bound to the old Law than a woman is to her dead husband.

Paul concludes his argument by saying, "You also have been made dead to the law through the body of Christ so that you might be joined to another, to Him who has been raised from the dead...but now we have been discharged from the law, having died to that in which we were held, so that we serve in newness of spirit and not in oldness of letter."[144] The oldness of letter is the Law, and we are dead to it and its mandates.

---

[143] Luke 5:39
[144] Romans 7:1-6

We have been discharged from law, freed from it, and dead to it. We have no right to command a Christian, who is dead to the old Law, to obey that Law's obsolete commands. We are free from the Law in every sense. It has no authority over those in Christ.

A Better Champion

"For the law was given through Moses; grace and reality came through Jesus Christ."[145] In contrast to the Mosaic Law, an external list of Dos and Don'ts, the Son of God offered a system of mercy based upon the truth of God's love. Rather than the Law's oppressive and exhausting yoke, Jesus said, "Come to Me all who toil and are burdened, and I will give you rest. Take My yoke upon you and learn from Me, for I am meek and lowly in heart, and you will find rest for your souls. For My yoke is easy and My burden is light."[146] To all those who have repeatedly tried to live up to God's standard through sheer willpower alone, God's only begotten Son offers a peace that comes from knowing our justification does not rest upon our own performance.

That is why the good news of God's kingdom was first preached to the Jews. Having been exposed to God's holiness and His demand for perfection, the Jews, of all peoples, would appreciate this new wine, this new economy that involved more than keeping some external command. The gospel promised rest from daily law keeping and freedom from a legal system that offered no hope. That's why it's the good news of the kingdom and its King, Jesus Christ.

---

[145] John 1:17
[146] Matthew 11:28-30 & 11:13

From Genesis 3 and forward, God promised to crush man's adversary and establish His reign upon the earth. He would "raise up to David a righteous Shoot. And He will reign as King."[147] Because this King would be resurrected, His "throne will be established forever."[148] "This One, having offered one sacrifice for sin, sat down forever on the right hand of God. Henceforth waiting until His enemies are made the footstool for His feet."[149] He intercedes for His people as "a Priest forever according to the order of Melchizedek."[150] All of the prophets, all of the angels, and all of creation watched to see how God would accomplish His will.[151] Even "Abraham exulted that he would see My day, and he saw it and rejoiced."[152] As the Son of God proclaimed, "The time is fulfilled and the kingdom of God has drawn near. Repent and believe in the gospel."[153]

The Jews had heard of Isaiah's Servant of whom it is written, "Surely, He has borne our sicknesses and carried our sorrows, yet we ourselves esteemed Him stricken, smitten of God and afflicted. But He was wounded because of our transgressions. He was crushed because of our iniquities. The chastening for our peace was upon

---

[147] Jeremiah 23:5
[148] 2 Samuel 7:16
[149] Hebrews 10:12-13
[150] Psalm 110:4
[151] See 1 Peter 1:10-12; Romans 8:19
[152] John 8:56
[153] Mark 1:15

Him, and by His stripes we have been healed."[154] And like the Ethiopian, they wondered who was mentioned, "As a sheep He was led to slaughter, and as a lamb before its shearer is dumb, so He does not open His mouth. In His humiliation His judgment was taken away. Who shall declare His generation? For His life is taken away from the earth."[155]

God promised Israel, "I will set up over them one Shepherd, My Servant David, and He will feed them; He will feed them, and He will be their Shepherd. And I, Jehovah, will be their God, and My Servant David will be a Prince among them. I, Jehovah, have spoken. And I will make with them a covenant of peace."[156] Jesus fulfilled this promise and declared, "I am the good Shepherd, the good Shepherd lays down His life for the sheep."[157] And because of His willing obedience to the Father, God exalted Him by "seating Him at His right hand in the heavenlies, far above all rule and authority and power and lordship and every name this is named."[158]

What the Israelites never imagined is how the LORD's Anointed, the Messiah,[159] would fulfill all the Law's requirements "for the whole law is fulfilled in one word,

---

[154] Isaiah 53:4-5
[155] Acts 8:32-33, Isaiah 53:7-8
[156] Ezekiel 34:23-24
[157] John 10:11
[158] Ephesians 1:20-21
[159] John 1:25, 1:41, 4:25, 7:26, 7:41

in this, 'You shall love your neighbor as yourself."[160]
Jesus was the perfect demonstration of the Law for He
loved God and loved others perfectly. They didn't realize
that Israel's new King would also be the Servant and "the
Lamb of God who takes away the sin of the world."[161]
They, like many today, didn't catch that Jesus' ministry
was a ministry of fulfillment.

Throughout the gospels, and especially in Matthew's (it
being written to the Jews), it repeatedly states, "so that
the Scripture might be fulfilled."[162] Being so familiar
with these texts, we normally just glace right over them,
but the recorders of Christ's ministry knew that the
testimony of the Law and prophets was extremely
significant. Because of the witness of the Law and
prophets, the actions of Jesus have eternal significance. If
Jesus had just died and raised from the dead apart from
the Old Testament prophecies, even His resurrection
would lose its implication. However, the Law and
prophets foretold, "You will not abandon my soul to
Hades, nor will You permit Your Holy One see
corruption."[163]

Jesus made it clear that the only sign He would give that
generation was the sign of Jonah in saying, "a sign shall

[160] Galatians 6:14
[161] John 1:29
[162] Matthew 1:22, 2:15-17, 2:23, 4:14, 5:18, 8:17, 12:17,
13:14, 13:35, 21:4, 26:54-56, 27:9, 27:35
[163] Acts 2:27 (Psalms 16:10)

not be given...except the sign of Jonah the prophet. For just as Jonah was in the belly of the great fish three days and three nights, so will the Son of Man be in the heart of the earth three days and three nights."[164]   And since Christ has been raised from dead, He is declared and proven to be the Holy One of God, and "through this One forgiveness of sins is announced to you; And from all the things from which you were not able to be justified by the law of Moses, in this One everyone who believes is justified."[165]

It's important to recognize that the Law pointed to Christ. Jesus confronted the religious leaders of His day who thought that through exact commandment keeping they would guarantee salvation when He said, "You search the Scriptures, because you think that in them you have eternal life; and it is these that testify concerning Me."[166] Every commandment of the Law was preparatory for the new wine of teaching that God's only Son would bring as He said, "Do not think that I have come to abolish the law or the prophets; I have not come to abolish, but to fulfill. For truly I say to you, Until heaven and earth pass away, one iota or one serif shall by no means pass away from the law until all come to pass. Therefore whoever annuls one of the least of these commandments, and teaches men so, shall be called the least in the kingdom of the heavens; but whoever practices and teaches them, he shall be

---

[164] Matthew 12:39-40
[165] Acts 13:38-39
[166] John 5:39

called great in the kingdom of the heavens. For I say to you that unless your righteousness surpasses that of the scribes and Pharisees, you shall by no means enter into the kingdom of the heavens."[167]

Already by the time Jesus preached the infamous Sermon on the Mount, Jesus' opponents had already accused Him of trying to destroy the Law. However, He says, "Do not think that I have come to abolish the law or the prophets; I have not come to abolish but to fulfill."[168] Jesus states His position in the negative and then in the positive. He says negatively, "I have not come to abolish," and positively, "but to fulfill." Before we examine what exactly He meant, it is necessary we understand Jesus' statement in its context. Jesus was speaking to Jews, those by birth who were subject to the Law given through Moses. He was declaring to everyone that His intent was never to destroy or annul the Law's commandments which His opponents were obviously accusing Him of doing.

Jesus cements His claim of supporting the Law by saying, "For truly I say to you, Until heaven and earth pass away, one iota and one serif shall by no means pass away from the law until all come to pass."[169] This statement must be understood as the supporting premise of His defense that He was not trying to abolish the Law. Note the word

---

[167] Matthew 5:17-20
[168] Matthew 5:17
[169] Matthew 5:18

66

"for" which begins verse 18. The word "for" means "because" and should signal to the audience that what preceded the "for" is the reason the conclusion is true, that He came to fulfill the law. He bases His position (of not being contrary to the Law) by stating the fact that the Law will never pass away until heaven and earth pass away. The Law will exist until the fulfillment of all its promises and prophecies "come to pass." But does the reality of the Law's existence mean that all believers are bound to obey its mandates for all eternity?[170]

The Law will exist until heaven and earth pass away, but this passage does not tell us in what capacity it will exist. It is presumptuous to assert that if a law exists it is binding upon everyone. Ask yourself this: Should citizens of the United States still keep the laws of Great

---

[170] When reading a text, especially when it is Scripture, it's important to note what the speaker says and doesn't say. What we think a statement may imply may not be necessarily true because implication is many times dependent upon the interpreter. It is presumptuous to assert our own agenda onto a text and dangerous to presuppose a doctrine that a text may not explicitly teach. There are thousands of misrepresentations of Christian doctrine based on one verse. These ideas remove passages from their written context and conveniently ignore the sum total of Scripture. There are also countless other misguided teachings founded upon human philosophy wherein the interpreter reads into a text what it doesn't necessarily say. Philosophical arguments have the appearance of wisdom, but what is or isn't true about God can only be confidently known through revelation.

Britain? Of course not! U.S. citizens are free from the laws of their old government just as Christians are free from the law God commanded the Israelites. In the same way, through Christ "we have been discharged from the Law, having died to that in which we were held, so that we serve in newness of spirit and not in oldness of letter."[171]

Some will still assert that because the Law is in existence it must be binding, but we know from Paul "that the law is not enacted for a righteous man but for the lawless and unruly, for the ungodly and sinners, for the unholy and profane, for those who strike their fathers and those..."[172] It does not exist for those with faith in Christ. Jesus does not, nor did any New Testament writer following Christ's resurrection, say that the Old Law is binding upon believers. Such a position contradicts the rest of the New Testament canon and it puts Jesus at odds with Peter and Paul, both apostles of His own choosing. Thus, we cannot assert that this is what Christ meant for if the sum of God's word does not support such a conjecture we must reject it and determine to find a position that harmonizes the totality of Scripture.

If we can grasp the overall point of Jesus' defense, that He came to fulfill the Law, then we can appreciate that "God, sending His own Son in the likeness of the flesh of sin and concerning sin condemned sin in the flesh, that

---

[171] Romans 7:6
[172] 1 Timothy 1:9

the righteous requirement of the [Mosaic] law might be fulfilled in us, who do not walk according to the flesh but according to the spirit."[173] Jesus is not tearing down the Law by fulfilling it, nor do those who walk according to the spirit annul it. Rather, those who worry about obeying every little detail of the Law fail to appreciate how Jesus' life and teachings fulfilled all the Law's requirements. They forget that Christ wiped out the "ordinances, which was against us; and He has taken it out of the way, nailing it to the cross."[174]

Yet, Jesus does say that "whoever annuls one of the least of these commandments, and teaches men so, shall be called the least in the kingdom of the heavens; but whoever practices and teaches them, he shall be called great in the kingdom of the heavens."[175] It does seem that Jesus is advocating strict obedience to the Law, but, again, this statement must be understood how Jesus always interpreted the Law.

This conclusion of who is great or least in the kingdom is not only based upon Christ's promise to fulfill the Law but also on the fact that "unless your righteousness surpasses that of the scribes and Pharisees, you shall by no means enter into the kingdom of the heavens."[176] Jesus shockingly points out that the scribes and Pharisees

---

[173] Romans 8:4
[174] Colossians 2:14
[175] Matthew 5:19
[176] Matthew 5:20

were not righteous. These religious leaders thought that by simply obeying the Law's rules they would achieve righteousness, but Jesus asserts that their understanding and application of the Law fell short of God's intent and their definition of righteousness was fundamentally wrong. He states that by keeping the Law, attempting to justify yourself through this list of rules, one will never gain admission into God's kingdom. "For Christ is the end of the law unto righteousness to everyone who believes."[177]

Jesus will show from this verse forward that His understanding and teaching of the Law are in complete accordance with the Law and are, in fact, God's true purpose for and interpretation of the Law. Jesus follows these statements with the true meaning behind and undergirding the Law. He exposes the inadequacy of the Law's external mandates, its concessions for man's wickedness, and its feeble attempt to control of one's flesh.

When Jesus pointed out to the Jews God's original intent for marriage, they were shocked. He said, "But I say to you that whoever divorces his wife, except for fornication, and marries another, commits adultery; and he who marries her who has been divorced commits adultery."[178] People like to think marriage is merely an agreement between them and their spouse and they have

---

[177] Romans 10:4
[178] Matthew 19:9

the right to annul this contract whenever they feel so inclined. The Jews thought that the Law's permission to divorce meant that it was acceptable in God's eyes. But Jesus points out that "because of your hardness of heart, [Moses] allowed you to divorce your wives, but from the beginning it has not been so."[179]

Jesus always taught in contrast to "you have heard that it was said" with "But I say to you." He confronted tradition and a childish view of the Law by showing that one's hatred for his brother was just as loathsome to God as the one who murders,[180] and the man who lusts was as culpable as the adulterer.[181] Jesus pointed out that the love of money is incompatible with a love for God.[182] He revealed how the quest for the acclaim of others was an affront to God.[183] He taught that a fruitless life, a saltless salt, a dark light, were worthless to the world or the Father.[184]

Our Lord and Savior spent much of His ministry correcting the leaven of the Pharisees, a base and fleshly view of the Law. He showed time and time again that the Law's mandates were written that we might understand God's true objective. When the Law commanded an "eye

---

[179] Matthew 19:8
[180] Matthew 5:22
[181] Matthew 5:28
[182] Matthew 6:19-24; Luke 16:13
[183] Matthew 6:1; Luke 11:43, 20:46-47
[184] Matthew 21:19, 5:13-16

for eye, tooth for tooth, hand for hand, foot for foot,"[185] God was really condemning vengeance. When Jesus said that "everything that enters from outside into a man is not able to defile him, Because it does not enter into his heart, but into the stomach, and goes out into the drain,"[186] He was showing that one should be more concerned about what goes in and comes out of one's heart. And even when the Law prescribed a day of rest, God was hoping His people would use this freedom to do good as Jesus said, "It is lawful to do well on the Sabbath."[187]

Just as the scribes and Pharisees of Jesus' day, teachers today who instruct people to obey the Law in hopes it will better justify them are the very ones who annul the Law they allegedly support. Churches who demand a tenth from those who can barely feed their family are no different than the Pharisees who condemned the disciples for rubbing grain in their hand. Believers who condemn others for working on the Sabbath have the same attitude of those who condemned Jesus for healing on a Saturday. Denominations that judge Christians who do not obey the Law are just like the Judaizers of Paul's day, "who stole in to spy out our freedom which we have in Christ Jesus, that they might bring us into slavery."[188] And any Christian who exalts himself in his perfect adherence to the Law is no different that the Pharisee who looked

---

[185] Exodus 21:24
[186] Mark 7:18-19
[187] Matthew 12:12
[188] Galatians 2:4

down on the publican and prayed, "Thank you that I am not like the rest of men."[189]

By now we should have come to realize that the Law of Moses was simply the bridge to a better way, "the child conductor"[190] to lead us to THE Teacher, Jesus Christ. The nature God desired His people to possess can never be attained by solely keeping an external rule.[191] The Mosaic Law's purpose was to instruct us towards righteousness, help mankind experientially feel their need for a Savior, and direct man towards the most important principles of love for God and love for others.

The Law of Moses falls so incredibly short of forming God's character within His people. It is a legal system, simply concerned with immediate justice. But the Law of Christ teaches us "not to resist him who is evil; rather...turn to him the other [cheek] also...to him who ask of you, give," to "love your enemies and pray for those who persecute you."[192] The Law had no concern with unwarranted mercy, especially to love those who hate us. The Law does not teach us how to love God with all our

---

[189] Luke 18:11

[190] Galatians 3:25-26

[191] It especially could not be handing down from one's parentage as even John said, "And do not presume to say within yourselves, We have Abraham as our father; for I tell you that God is able, out of these stones, to raise up children to Abraham."

[192] Matthew 5:38-48

heart, mind, soul and strength. Only His Son, Jesus, shows us how this can be done.

Just as a child is kept "under guardians and stewards until the time appointed by the father. So also we, when we were children, were kept in slavery under the elements of the world."[193]   Before Christ, we worried about every little detail, every lapse in judgment, and every good thing we did or didn't do. We made sure we looked good for church, said the right things, ate the right foods, associated with the right people, honored the right holy days, gave the right amount, et cetera, etc. And just like infantile children, we looked to the Law to tell us what was right and wrong.

Before Jesus came we were held captive by this mindset, but Christ was "born under law, that He might redeem those under law that we might receive the sonship."[194] We, of faith in Christ, are no longer under the Law's rules, its guardianship, for we are now adopted sons of God. Never forget that you cannot be redeemed from something unless you are its slave. The Law, even with all its good, was an oppressive system that required the death of God's son to save us from it. It's not that it was just replaced with a better system. The Law was and is a "ministry of death."[195] But thanks be to God that "since faith has come, we are no longer under a child conductor,

---

[193] Galatians 4:2-3
[194] Galatians 4:4-5
[195] 2 Corinthians 3:7

for you are all sons of God through faith in Christ Jesus."[196]

Jesus Christ is the absolute and final Teacher to whom we should listen. The same God whose voice shook the foundations of Mt. Sinai, told His people later, "This is My Son, the Beloved. Hear Him."[197] In contrast to Moses, the Lawgiver, and Elijah, the greatest of the prophets, Jesus is only One to whom we should listen. Christ is THE Prophet to whom God commanded we listen "for He has been counted worthy of more glory than Moses, by as much as He who built the house has more honor than the house."[198] And "there is salvation in no other, for neither is there another name under heaven given among men in which we must be saved."[199]

Jesus' comprehension of God's will goes so much farther than the Law could ever reach. Rather than "An eye for an eye, and a tooth for a tooth" Jesus commands His disciples to "turn to him the other [cheek] also"[200] and to "Love your enemies, and pray for those who persecute you."[201] Just as God causes the rain to fall on the unrighteous, we should love our enemies who despise and oppress us. Our Lord defined the neighbor whom we are

---

[196] Galatians 3:25-26
[197] Mark 9:7
[198] Hebrews 3:3
[199] Acts 4:12
[200] Matthew 5:38-39
[201] Matthew 5:44

75

to love,[202] and died for every one of His enemies. His life is a perfect demonstration of what loving God with all your heart, mind, and strength looks like. And He exceeded the mandate to love others as yourself, but declared, "This is My commandment, that you love one another even as I have loved you."[203] And how much did He love us? Enough to lay down His life.

Jesus' life and death are the most perfect display of God's hatred of sin and His love for the sinner. As the Father allowed His Son to be beaten, mocked, spat on, and hanged to die we see the heinousness of sin. How much greater is this demonstration of God's wrath toward sin than some rule in the Law? God's wrath and judgment of sin is more fully demonstrated in the crucifixion and death of His Son than in any legal commandment. In Christ's death we have the perfect display of God's grace and mercy toward the sinner. God's Son hanged bleeding on a Roman cross until the full penalty for sin was paid and His Father's wrath against sin was satisfied as His Son, Himself, said, "It is finished."[204]

And through Christ's death we realize how very much He loved us. The just recompense for our sins was fully exercised on His Son. "Scarcely for a righteous man will anyone die...but God commends His own love to us in

---

[202] Luke 10:25-37
[203] John 15:12
[204] John 19:30

that while we were yet sinners, Christ died for us."[205] No one would wish their own child die in the place of an enemy. Yet God, being rich in mercy, permitted the humiliation and sacrifice of His Son to atone for the evil we have done. There is no logical argument for what God did. He illogical loves us, sinners.

No preaching of the Law, of its greatness or morality, can ever attain to the message of the cross. The Law falls short to the glory of the gospel. It is the good news of God, that Jesus Christ was crucified, and through it God "might be righteous and the One who justifies him who is of the faith of Jesus."[206] It is only through Christ's death and resurrection that sinners like you and I can be justified before God. The perfect life and death of Christ is a better sermon than any exegesis of the Law. He is the good shepherd who gives up His life for His sheep. He is the "bread of life" that "come down out of heaven and gives life to the world."[207] He is the living water so that "whoever drinks of the water that I will give him shall by no means thirst forever."[208] He is the way, the truth and life "and no one comes to the Father except through Me."[209]

---

[205] Romans 5:7-8
[206] Romans 3:26
[207] John 6:33-35
[208] John 4:14
[209] See John 14:6

A Better Counselor

"All Scripture is God-breathed and profitable for teaching, for conviction, for correction, for instruction in righteousness, that the man of God may be complete, fully equipped for every good work."[210] Scripture in this passage refers to the Old Testament, and, as mentioned previously, the Law does have its usefulness. On the other hand, we never witness a New Testament disciple utilizing the Mosaic Law to point out people's sins and then proceed to preach Christ crucified. When speaking to Jews, they did appeal to the Law to show in what way this Jesus of Nazareth fulfilled the Law's prophecies and how He, being Christ and Lord, demanded their obedience to Him. But the chosen ministers of Jesus Christ never first preached the Law's moral mandates to either Jews or Greeks.

The apostles of Christ began preaching from wherever the person was at in their search to know God. If a seeker was reading the Old Testament, then Philip began with that verse. If they were an Athenian who prided themselves in their spirituality, Paul began with their understanding of those gods. "And to the Jews I became as a Jew in order that I might gain Jews; to those under law, as under law (though I myself am not under law), that I might gain those under law. To those without law, as without law (though I am not without law to God but

---

[210] 2 Timothy 3:16-17

within law to Christ), that I might gain those without law. To the weak I became weak that I might gain the weak. To all men I have become all things that I might by all means save some."[211] From Paul and every New Testament example, we learn the best method of evangelism is to start on common ground rather than trying to appeal to or force a Law upon people who do not know it nor recognize its authority.

Yes, you can preach the Ten Commandments to the lost, but, keep in mind, most people naturally obey much of the Law without even realizing it. Because man is made in God's image,[212] with the imprint of the Creator residing in their spirit and conscience, people instinctively know that murder is wrong, greed is wrong, adultery is wrong, stealing is wrong, lying is wrong, etc. As it is written, "For when Gentiles, who have no law, do by nature the things of the law, these, though they have no law, are a law to themselves, who show the work of the law written in their hearts, their conscience bearing witness with it and their reasonings, one with the other, accusing or even excusing them.[213]

It is even possible to keep the Law's commandments, to be moral, and yet still be far away from God. Did not the Pharisees prove that one could keep the Law's mandates and still be unrighteous? Isn't it much easier to obey a

---

[211] 1 Corinthians 9:20-22
[212] Genesis 1:26-27
[213] Romans 2:14-15

list of "Thou shalls" and "Thou shall nots" than to fully submit to Christ as Lord? You see? We can force the world to act moral, to look like Christians, who "outwardly appear righteous" but "inwardly are full of dead men's bones...full of hypocrisy and lawlessness."[214] In fact, we can accept them into fellowship, ensure they faithfully attend service, and collect their weekly tithe, but that still doesn't make them any more saved than they were before. As the old expression goes, *"Just because you sit in a hen house, doesn't make you a chicken."* A person can repent of sinful acts and never repent of one's own lordship. They can appear born again and still be dead to God. They may even keep all of the Law's commands, but if not coupled with faith it will profit them nothing[215]because "without faith it is impossible to be well pleasing to Him."[216]

In many of our churches, we want to skip the ugly and difficult message of repentance and self-crucifixion, that our Lord demanded His disciple to "deny himself and take up his cross and follow Me."[217] We ignore the evils of self-centeredness, self-sufficiency, self-esteem and prefer to just discuss how much God loves us. People can never appreciate the good news of Jesus Christ unless they fully comprehend the bad news of their position. With the same inclination, we readily preach the Ten

---

[214] Matthew 23:27-28

[215] See Romans 9:30-32

[216] Hebrews 11:6

[217] Matthew 16:24

Commandments because they are, in fact, easy. But to hold back our tongue, to consider others greater than ourselves, to pray for our enemies, to bless those who persecute us, to give up all our possessions, to leave the comforts of home and serve those less fortunate, to let others sue us and take our belongings, now "This word is hard; who can hear it?"[218]

And even though the Law can never match the power of the gospel of Jesus Christ we should not assume that the gospel is all a preacher would ever need. Man is inherently wicked and a mere list of historical proofs will never move one to godly repentance. This is why our Lord promised a helper, a comforter, a counselor who would come and "when He comes, He will convict the world concerning sin and concerning righteousness and concerning judgment: Concerning sin because they do not believe into Me; And concerning righteousness because I am going to the Father and you no longer hold Me; And concerning judgment because the ruler of this world has been judged."[219]

The world isn't condemned because they fail to keep the Ten Commandments. They are guilty because they do not believe in Christ. As the Scripture says, "he who does not believe has been condemned already, because he has not believed into the name of the only begotten Son

---

[218] John 6:60
[219] John 16:8-11

of God."[220] They are declared unrighteous because Jesus is raised and sits at the right hand of the Father as Lord. They are judged because their father, Satan, has been proven a liar, and like their representative, Adam, they willing choose to become one's own god. This autonomous lordship was fully manifested as genuine hatred toward God in the death of Christ. Never be misled. The world hates God with the same passion that nailed His innocent Son to a cross and gladly watching Him suffer crucifixion. It is this spirit of the world that is condemned, not just their wicked deeds.

And just as the message of the cross is exceedingly more powerful than an appeal to the Law so is the Spirit far more effective in the conviction of man than any list of written commandments. The living and breathing Spirit of God is far more superior in convicting the world than the dead Law of Moses could ever hope to attain. Just as the ear has been designed to hear the gospel, man's conscience is perfectly made to be convicted of sin.

God's Holy Spirit goes far beyond simply convicting the world of sin. He searches man's heart[221] and is given to all those who believe, repent and are baptized.[222] Through the Spirit all disciples, both Jew and Gentile, are

---

[220] John 3:18

[221] Romans 8:27, 1 Corinthians 2:10

[222] Acts 2:38, 1 Corinthians 3:16, Galatians 3:14, 1 Thessalonians 4:8, 1 John 3:24, 4:13

baptized into one body, the church.[223] "For through Him we both have access in one Spirit unto the Father."[224] He intercedes for the saints[225] and "witnesses with our spirit that we are children of God."[226] The Spirit distributes gifts "to each one respectively even as He purposes."[227] It is the Spirit that implants the covenant's laws[228], the "law of the Spirit"[229] "not in tablets of stone but in tablets of hearts"[230] so that we might be led and walk according to the spirit[231] and produce its fruit[232] for "if you are led by the Spirit you are not under Law."[233] He is given as our resurrection guarantee, God's pledge to us, that we have eternal life.[234] The Spirit, the Comforter, is superior to the old Law in every way.

---

[223] 1 Corinthians 12:13
[224] Ephesians 2:18
[225] Romans 8:27
[226] Romans 8:16 (see also Romans 8:9)
[227] 1 Corinthians 12:11
[228] Jeremiah 31:33
[229] Romans 8:2
[230] 2 Corinthians 3:3
[231] Romans 8:4, 14
[232] Galatians 5:22-23
[233] Galatians 5:18
[234] Romans 8:11, 2 Corinthians 1:22, 2 Corinthians 5:5, Ephesians 1:13-14

Who is to Obey the New Law?

Even after Christ had instituted a new covenant in His blood and had been raised from the dead, His disciples still did not fully comprehend the nature or the vastness of His kingdom. Evidently they thought Jesus would restore the kingdom to Israel immediately.[235]

However, Jesus had already insinuated that the kingdom would no longer belong solely to the Jew. He said, "Therefore I say to you that the kingdom of God shall be taken from you and shall be given to a nation producing its fruit."[236] God had held out His hand to a disobedient and stiff-necked people for hundreds of years. They had rejected "the stone which was considered as nothing by you, the builders."[237] Christ lamented the sad situation of His people by human descent saying, "Jerusalem, Jerusalem, who kills the prophets and stones those who are sent to her! How often I desired to gather your children together, the way a hen gathers her brood under her wings, and you would not!"[238] God had invited them to the feast, yet they refused to come.[239] So God sent His servants into the streets, into the world of the filthy Gentiles.

---

[235] Acts 1:6
[236] Matthew 21:43
[237] Acts 4:11
[238] Matthew 23:37
[239] Matthew 22:1-14

That God would accept a Gentile without first being circumcised was not appreciated until the conversion of Cornelius. It was incomprehensible that a Gentile could be justified by God apart from any acknowledgement of the Law. For assuredly, Gentiles "were apart from Christ, alienated from the commonwealth of Israel, and strangers to the covenants of the promise, having no hope and without God in the world."[240] So, at the time, it is completely unknown that God would extend His forgiveness to the nations, those who had never even heard of Him, apart from Israel.

And yet God had kept "the mystery which has been hidden from the ages and from the generations but now has been manifested to His saints, to whom God willed to make known what are the riches of the glory of this mystery among the Gentiles, which is Christ in you, the hope of glory."[241] Sadly, many Christians today will explain away illogical arguments by stating that, *"It's just a mystery."* But a mystery, by definition, is not something we cannot understand. A mystery is simply what is not revealed yet as it says, "The things that are hidden belong to Jehovah our God; but the things that are revealed, to us and our children forever."[242] So it's not that the mystery of Christ dwelling in Gentiles is incomprehensible. It is merely that it was never imagined or known to mankind until God chose to reveal it.

---

[240] Ephesians 2:12
[241] Colossians 1:26-27
[242] Deuteronomy 29:29

The revelation is that Christ, God's Beloved and Chosen One, His Servant, the true Shepherd of His people would be the One through whom all the Gentiles would be justified.[243] As it says, "I have given You as a covenant for the people, as a light for the nations; To open the eyes of the blind, To bring the prisoner out from the prison, Those who dwell in darkness from the prison house."[244] Jesus, Himself, would be the covenant, the Light of the world who calls anyone and everyone out of darkness. Those who believe into Him would be justified, accounted righteous, before God through faith, apart from the old covenant. God would be propitiated, His wrath against sin would be satisfied, by the atonement achieved through the sacrifice of His own Son, Jesus Christ. And Gentiles would be equal partners of a new covenant so that "now in Christ Jesus you who were once far off have become near in the blood of Christ."[245]

Jesus Christ "is our peace, He who has made both [Jew and Gentile] one and has broken down the middle wall of partition, the enmity, abolishing in His flesh the law of the commandments in ordinances, that He might create the two in Himself into one new man, so making peace. And might reconcile both in one Body to God through the cross, having slain the enmity by it."[246] The enmity, the

---

[243] See Isaiah 11:10, 42:1,6, 49:6, 62:2, 65:1,15
[244] Isaiah 42:6-7
[245] Ephesians 2:12
[246] Ephesians 2:15

contempt of the Jew for the Gentile and of the Gentile for the Jew, was destroyed by Christ's death. The church, the disciples of Christ, would not be an offshoot, or some sect, of Judaism. "There is no distinction"[247] between the faithful Jew and the Gentile of faith because God "does not regard persons."[248] He has taken people out of Judaism and out of heathenism to create the assembly of God, the living body of Christ.

Even though "God first visited the Gentiles to take out from them a people for His name,"[249] the Jews misappropriately held their heads in pride because they were "the sons of the prophets and of the covenant."[250] But no longer could a Hebrew possess sole claim of being God's chosen people merely on account of their earthly forefathers. Every believer, even the Israelite, had to be "born anew"[251] "not of blood..., but of God"[252] into a new heavenly kingdom. Their citizenship would no longer rest on earth.[253] Their home was not just some pile of dirt in Canaan, but an abode with Christ as He promised, "I go to prepare a place for you. And if I go and prepare a place for you, I am coming again and will receive you to

---

[247] Romans 3:21-22
[248] Deuteronomy 10:17
[249] Acts 15:14
[250] Acts 3:25
[251] John 3:3
[252] John 1:13
[253] See Philippians 3:20

Myself, so that where I am you also may be."[254]
"Therefore the inheritance is out of faith that it might be according to grace, so that the promise may be certain to all the seed."[255]

The promises made to Abraham were never annulled by the Law. "It is not the children of the flesh who are the children of God, but the children of the promise are accounted as the seed."[256] Those who believe into God through Christ are sons of believing Abraham. They are the true seed, not just those who are physically descended from Abraham. "God is not a respecter of persons, but in every nation he who fears Him and works righteousness is acceptable to Him."[257] It is not just the Jew who can be acceptable to God. It is not just those who are circumcised or those who obey the Law, but "everyone who believes into Him will receive forgiveness of sins."[258]

This is why Jesus told His apostles to "Go therefore and disciple all the nations, baptizing them into the name of the Father and of the Son and of the Holy Spirit,"[259] "that repentance for forgiveness of sins would be proclaimed in

---

[254] John 14:2-3
[255] Romans 4:15-16
[256] Romans 9:8
[257] Acts 10:34-35
[258] Acts 10:43
[259] Matthew 28:19

His name to all the nations."[260] This new covenant people would be "a chosen race, a royal priesthood, a holy nation"[261] "called by a new name, which the mouth of Jehovah will designate."[262] It would be "built upon the foundation of the apostles and the prophets, Christ Jesus Himself being the cornerstone."[263] The Gentile had been "grafted in" the place of the unbelieving Jew.[264] They were the truly circumcised, for their circumcision was "of the heart, in spirit, not in letter, whose praise if not from men, but from God."[265]

Unlike the covenant that God made with the Israelites on Mt. Sinai, the new covenant initiated by the death of Christ is available to everyone, Jew and Gentile alike. "As He also says in Hosea, "I will call those who were not My people My people, and her who was not beloved beloved. And it shall be that in the place where it was said to them, You are not My people, there shall they be called sons of the living God."[266] Indeed, you will call a nation that you do not know, And a nation that does not know you will run to you, Because of Jehovah your God, even the Holy One of Israel, for He has glorified You."[267] And again God says, "I let Myself be inquired of by those

---

[260] Luke 24:47
[261] 1 Peter 2:9
[262] Isaiah 62:2
[263] Ephesians 2:20
[264] See Romans 11:17-20
[265] Romans 2:29
[266] Romans 9:25-26
[267] Isaiah 55:5

who did not ask for Me, And found by those who did not seek Me. I said, Here I am; here I am; To a nation that was not called by My name."[268]

"Being then the race of God,...[He] having overlooked the times of ignorance, God now charges all men everywhere to repent. Because He has set a day in which He is to judge the world in righteousness by the Man whom He has designated, having furnished proof to all by raised Him from the dead."[269] Because this new covenant is available to everyone, those who choose to reject God's gift of salvation remain under condemnation as it is written, "He who believes into Him is not condemned; but he who does not believe has been condemned already, because he has not believed into the name of the only begotten Son of God."[270]

However, "The Lord...is longsuffering toward you, not intending that any perish but that all advance to repentance. But the day of the Lord will come as a thief."[271] Just as the homeowner has no warning when a thief plans to break into his home, no one will know when Christ returns for "no one knows, not even the angels of the heavens nor the Son."[272] And just as the wicked ignored Noah's preaching, just as they carried on about

---

[268] Isaiah 65:1
[269] Acts 17:29-31
[270] John 3:18
[271] 2 Peter 3:9-10
[272] Matthew 24:36

their lives mocking him as he "prepared an ark for the salvation of his house,"[273] those who are too distracted, too in love with wickedness will miss out on such a great salvation. "How shall we escape if we have neglected so great a salvation?"[274] But praise be to our God who is patient, waiting until every last soul has had to opportunity to turn to Him. That is why "now is the well-acceptable time...now is the day of salvation."[275]

---

[273] Hebrews 11:7, see also Matthew 24:37-38 & Luke 17:26-27
[274] Hebrews 2:3
[275] 2 Corinthians 6:2

Why is the New Law Better?

"For by grace you have been saved through faith, and this not of yourselves; it is the gift of God; not of works that no one should boast. For we are His masterpiece, created in Christ Jesus for good works, which God prepared beforehand in order that we would walk in them."[276]

God's gift of forgiveness, of redemption, of reconciliation, of adoption as sons, of an eternal inheritance is achieved via the means of grace. God's love is the principal motivation and His grace offered through His Son is the avenue by which God chooses to save mankind. At no time, past or present, have we done enough to merit this grace, to compel God to give us what we never deserved. It is solely because God is loving and gracious that we have the opportunity to accept this salvation available solely through Jesus Christ's death and resurrection.

This does not mean, however, that we live free of any obligation, that we can continue to sin and think we have not forfeited this great gift. As the Scripture says, "Should we continue in sin that grace may abound? Absolutely not! We who have died to sin, how shall we still live in it?"[277] Contrary to what may be popular, God's grace is not a license to sin. Our reconciliation to

---

[276] Ephesians 2:8-10
[277] Romans 6:1-2

God is conditional, not only on our acceptance of His grace on His terms (not ours), but also on our obedience to "walk in the light as He is in the light." It is only those who continue this walk who are promised that "the blood of Jesus His Son cleanses us from every sin."[278] And yet it is not the perfection of our walk but the act of walking by which we retain our fellowship with Him.

On the day of judgment, you and I can be presented as "holy and without blemish and without reproach before Him; If indeed you continue in the faith, grounded and steadfast and not being moved away from the hope of the gospel."[279] The difference for the Christian is that "sin will not lord it over you, for you are not under the law but under grace."[280] Those who live under the old Law are never free from the power and reign of sin, but those who are "buried with Him through baptism"[281] are free from its lordship and tyranny. Consequently, sin cannot command a Christian to obey any more than we can command a dead dog to sit.

Having died with Christ we are raised to "walk in newness of life."[282] We live in a state of freedom from the dominion of sin. It is impossible for those buried with Christ and dead to sin to be subject to it any longer. Sin

---

[278] 1 John 1:7
[279] Colossians 1:22-23
[280] Romans 6:14
[281] Romans 6:4
[282] Romans 6:4

is no longer our default master. Being "justified from sin,"[283] you now have to option to "present your members as weapons of unrighteousness to sin"[284] or to "present your members as slaves to righteousness unto sanctification."[285]

Within the economy of God's grace, there still exists a law. But the law of this administration is not "engraved in stone"[286] but a law written upon our hearts.[287] It is a law of the Spirit[288] that yields the fruit of the Spirit.[289] "For you were called for freedom, brothers; only do not turn this freedom into an opportunity for the flesh, but through love serve one another."[290] It is a new law that goes beyond the old commandment to love your neighbor as yourself, but to love one another as Christ loved us.[291] Just as saying *"I love you"* is meaningless if that love does not lead to action, so is saying *"I love God"* is hypocritical if it does not lead to good works. For Christ said, "If you love Me, you will keep My commandments,"[292] Accordingly, we cannot claim to

---

[283] Romans 6:7

[284] Romans 6:13

[285] Romans 6:19

[286] 2 Corinthians 3:7

[287] Jeremiah 31:33

[288] Romans 8:2

[289] See Galatians 5:22-26

[290] Galatians 5:13

[291] See John 15:12

[292] John 14:15

love God if we refuse to obey His Son for such a person "is a liar, and the truth is not in this one."[293]

Now I understand that this matter of obedience seems out of place for a discussion on the Law, but before we dive into how awesome and perfect God's gift is through Christ Jesus we must remember that "faith, if it does not have works, is dead in itself."[294] We must be cognizant to never swing the doctrinal pendulum too far to an extreme. History has shown that many theologians disproportionately react to false teaching by creating a contrary false teaching of their own, so we must be careful to never go beyond the revealed sum total of God's word.

Today, one side of Christendom argues our salvation is completely and solely an act of God while the other extreme posits that salvation is totally achievable by man. The former, then, makes God into an arbitrary monster who, without any reason, arbitrarily chooses to save some and condemn others while the latter negates the entire reason for which Christ died. Far be it from any of us to move beyond the balance that is explicit throughout Scripture.

---

[293] 1 John 2:4
[294] James 2:17

Christ can Free!

Freedom! It's a word we often hear but seldom understand. Being a relative term, freedom has various degrees of liberty. Americans, for example, like to believe they are free, but this freedom is still not immune to every law. One cannot do whatever one wants even in a *free* society. What we mean when we say, *"we are free"* is that we have a choice in certain aspects of our life. Freedom is an agreement between the governed and the government as to what areas of one's life he or she is able to exercise complete free choice. This is evident in where one chooses to buy food, find shelter, or even in what news provider one listens. However, one is not able to freely use the property of another, indiscriminately harm others, or refuse to pay taxes. One is not free to do whatever they want. So we see that freedom, by definition, is a subjective term wherein an individual has more or less choice under one government versus another.

This meaning is exactly how the New Testament understands our freedom in Christ when it says, "It is for freedom that Christ has set us free; Stand fast therefore, and do not be entangled with a yoke of slavery again."[295] It is not as though we are able to do whatever we want when we are in Christ for there is still "the law of Christ."[296] It means we are free from foolish "philosophy

---

[295] Galatians 5:1
[296] Galatians 6:2

and empty deceit, according to the tradition of men, according to the elements of the world, and not according to Christ."[297]

These worldly and man-made systems are easily identified. We know a teaching is not according to Christ whenever we hear, "Do not handle, nor taste, nor touch."[298] For some reason, mankind always seeks to pervert the freedom we have in Christ with additional rules that neither He nor His apostles ever commanded. And although "such things indeed have a reputation of wisdom in self-imposed worship and lowliness and severe treatment of the body, but are not of any value against the indulgence of the flesh."[299] It does seem highly spiritual to religiously obey the Sabbath, to observe special *"Christian"* holidays, to make vows before Passover, to abstain from certain foods, to advocate celibacy in our leaders, but all these are man's creation for the sole purpose of enslaving and judging Christ's followers. Thus, it is just as necessary today as it was 2000 years ago to tell our fellow brothers and sisters, "Let no one therefore judge you in eating and in drinking or in respect of a feast or of a new moon or of the Sabbath."[300]

---

[297] Colossians 2:8
[298] Colossians 2:21
[299] Colossians 2:23
[300] Colossians 2:16

The Law of Moses was a system that specified what you were and were not allowed to do, what you must and must not do, what customs and rituals you had to keep. As a subject to this Law, you did not have a choice to alter or amend any of it. You were bound to it and lived because you kept it. But the Law could go no farther. Since it was a system based upon external works, it could never reveal one's motive or the heart of the subject. There was no middle ground or system of grace when one failed to keep a commandment. There was no way to simply confess our sins and know that He would "forgive us our sins and cleanse us from all unrighteousness."[301]

But Christ died to free us from an external legal system. Unlike those subject to the Law, "There is now then no condemnation to those who are in Christ Jesus. For the law of the Spirit of life has freed me in Christ Jesus from the law of sin and of death."[302] Like a conqueror who invaded a land, "He led captive those taken captive and gave gifts to men."[303] Christ subjugated and conquered our enemies: sin and death. And the only way to do such was to remove and replace the Law that could never bring us freedom, never grant pardon, and never purify its offenders. His death and resurrection freed us from our nationalistic pride, our confidence in our good works, our love of self, and our reliance upon law keeping.

---

[301] 1 John 1:9
[302] Romans 8:1-2
[303] Ephesians 4:8

The old Law was helpless against the flesh because written laws operate through the flesh. The perfect intent and holiness of the Law was muted as it was filtered through our sinful flesh so that we, like Paul, "do not do the good which I will; but the evil which I do not will, this I practice."[304] The Law could only produce a harvest of spiritual fruit along with tares and weeds. Children need to be told by their parents what is right and wrong, so also spiritual children need the Law to explain what is good and bad. However, "the spiritual man discerns all things, but he himself is discerned by no one" because "we have the mind of Christ."[305]

Understand this: by telling Christians they should obey the old Law we are stealing their freedom. It is an attempt to bind upon them a burden that God never intended for His children. Christ died to set us free and "not be entangled with a yoke of slavery again."[306] Those who teach we need to obey the Law are either sorely misguided or even worse "false brothers, brought in secretly, who stole in to spy out our freedom which we have in Christ Jesus, that they might bring us into slavery."[307]

We, Christians, don't fight and murder because the Law tells us not to. We don't ridicule, gossip and slander just

---

[304] Romans 7:19
[305] 1 Corinthians 2:15-16
[306] Galatians 5:1
[307] Galatians 2:4

because it's wrong. The reason we don't do these things is because we love our neighbor, a soul for whom Christ died. We forgive because God also forgives us.[308] We even go so far as to pray for our enemies, for the very ones who persecute us.[309] We are free from doing the bare minimum to be just *good enough*. We are free to be led by the Spirit, to "grow up into Him in all things,"[310] and to "know the knowledge-surpassing love of Christ that we may be filled unto all the fullness of God."[311] And in doing so, we not only fulfill all the law's requirements but go beyond what the Law, with its limited scope, could ever force us to do.

When I help my wife with the dishes or laundry, I don't do it because I'm afraid she'll nag me to death. I do it because I love her, because she is my partner, my helper. Doing good for others because *we have to* will only yield modest results. We will do just enough to ease our conscience, to relieve the guilt every time the preacher tells us we should. We will give our tithe just to *shut him up*. However, if we truly love God and people, we automatically give and do whatever we can. We sell our possessions to give to those in need. We sacrifice our own needs to care for and serve others. We give up wasted time on entertainment and wash the dirty feet of sinners. We are free to love, to give, to care for, to

---

[308] See Matthew 6:14-15
[309] Matthew 5:44
[310] Ephesians 4:15
[311] Ephesians 3:19

encourage, to admonish, to discipline, and to forgive. These are "the good works, which God prepared beforehand in order that we would walk in them."[312] This is the type of church that will transform the world.

Now, I ask you, "having begun by the Spirit are you now being perfected by the flesh?"[313] In other words, you accepted the forgiveness and new life that comes through faith in Jesus Christ and are you now going to somehow become more forgiven, more saved, more born again by obeying the Law? Almost every Protestant denomination teaches justification through faith in Christ Jesus. And, yet, some will preach obedience to the Jewish Law. How contradictory and confusing! With one breath we say, *"You are saved on the basis of Christ,"* and with the very next breath we say, *"But you better keep the Ten Commandments or you're in grave spiritual danger."* How can such double talk exist within our churches?

So again I ask, "How is it that you turn again to the weak and poor elements, to which you desire to be enslaved again?"[314] What compels you to want to worry about perfect obedience to a system of dead works? Do you really want to live in a state of insecurity, always worrying that you're good enough, that you did enough, that God will be merciful enough to save your wretched soul? This kind of teaching is not good news. It is the

---

[312] Ephesians 2:10
[313] Galatians 3:3
[314] Galatians 4:9

opposite. It is "not another gospel."[315] It is the same *"pull yourself up by your own bootstraps"* ideology that permeates all of man's false religions. Don't be misled. Do not be deceived. This is not the good news of Christ. "As we have said before, now also I say again, If anyone announces to you a gospel beyond that which you have received, let him be accursed."[316]

"For you have not received a spirit of slavery [based on the Law] bringing you into fear again [because of your failures], but you have received a spirit of sonship [through your adoption] in which we cry, Abba, Father!"[317] When we are redeemed by God through Christ we are not just freed from sin and the law. We are adopted as His children. We are "born of water and Spirit."[318] It is not as if we did not exist prior to our new birth. Rather, we once lived in the realm of sin, but having been born again we now live in the realm of the Spirit. When we were "buried...with Him through baptism into His death in order that...we might walk in newness of life"[319] we are likewise transferred from "the authority of darkness and transferred us into the kingdom of the Son of His love."[320]

---

[315] Galatians 1:7
[316] Galatians 1:9
[317] Romans 8:14-15
[318] John 3:5
[319] Romans 6:4
[320] Colossians 1:13

Not only are we God's children now, but we are brothers of Jesus Christ for He raised Him up that "He might be the Firstborn among many brothers."[321] God didn't just save us to possess more subjects to do His bidding. He saved us to be His inheritance, His own family. As mind blowing as this is, in the resurrection, we, Christ's brothers, will be like Him as the word says, "It has not yet been manifested what we will be. We know that if He is manifested, we will be like Him because we will see Him even as He is."[322] And as siblings of God's only begotten Son, we enjoy all the blessings of our Father. Our eldest brother, Jesus Christ, sits at the right hand of God. He intercedes for the saints, meaning He intercedes for us! We are God's children and Christ Jesus' brothers and sisters.

It is no wonder, then, that we can boldly approach the throne of grace. His Spirit knows our spirit and "joins in to help us in our weakness...the Spirit Himself intercedes for us with groanings which cannot be uttered."[323] God's only begotten Son leans in towards the Great "I AM" and pleads our case. All of our worries and cares, hopes and dreams are ever present before the Father. Our big Brother ensures He hears us. Whatever we ask for in His name, He will ensure we receive because we have fellowship with the Father and the Son.[324]

---

[321] Romans 8:29
[322] 1 John 3:2
[323] Romans 8:26
[324] See John 14:13-14; 1 John 1:3

Christ can Justify!

The reality that no one can be truly righteous by law keeping was not lost on the first century Jew. And it is for this reason thousands of Israelites flocked to hear Christ's message of God's kingdom. The scribes and Pharisees of that era were not fond of this "new wine" for they reasoned "the old is better."[325] The Pharisees were undoubtedly considered the most righteous at that time. They not only separated themselves to obey all of the Mosaic Law, but also all of the traditions of their fathers. They went above and beyond the normal law keeping. Yet, Christ taught that "unless your righteousness surpasses that of the scribes and Pharisees, you shall by no means enter into the kingdom of the heavens."[326] How can this be?

"Because they pursued it not out of faith, but as it were out of works. They stumbled at the stone of stumbling."[327] What the Pharisee and many today don't fully comprehend is that our own righteousness is not enough. "All our righteousnesses are like a soiled garment"[328] before a holy God. What they and we should have learned from the Law is that "all have sinned and fall short of the glory of God."[329] No one, including the

---

[325] Luke 5:39

[326] Matthew 5:20

[327] Romans 9:32

[328] Isaiah 64:6

[329] Romans 3:23

Pope himself, can ever be righteous enough to be justified before God without the blood of Christ.

The Pharisees "were ignorant of God's righteousness and sought to establish their own righteousness, they were not subject to the righteousness of God. For Christ is the end of the law unto righteousness to everyone who believes."[330] When we turn to Christ in faith we are declaring that we have given up trying to establish our own righteousness. We acknowledge that we have fallen short and will continue to fall short of perfection, but we will not rest our faith in ourselves any longer. We place our trust in Christ: His life, death and resurrection, as the only means by which we can be justified.

This righteousness, God's righteousness, is solely based upon what Christ did. As it is written, "Him who did not know sin He made sin on our behalf that we might become the righteousness of God in Him."[331] Just as you cannot add oil to water and still have pure water, we cannot add God's righteousness to our unrighteousness and be declared righteous. Our unrighteousness must be completely replaced by God's righteousness. Because everyone who trusts in Christ is "found in Him, not having my own righteousness which is out of the law, but that which is through faith in Christ, the righteousness which is out of God and based on faith."[332]

---

[330] Romans 10:3-4
[331] 2 Corinthians 5:21
[332] Philippians 3:9

Righteousness must be accounted to us from Christ's account or it is never enough. It is through the imputation of God's righteousness, through our faith in God who supplies it, that we are justified. "To the one who does not work, but believes on Him who justifies the ungodly, his faith is accounted as righteousness."[333] The Mosaic Law could never justify one before God "for we account that a man is justified by faith apart from the works of the law."[334] We can't present our works, even perfect obedience to the Law, and then add Christ's work on the cross. We are justified apart from these works. "Apart" means they are exclusive of one another, not inclusive. Justification by faith is not a supplement for our works. It does not partner with our works to achieve justification. We are not justified through faith in addition to our good works. We are declared righteous before God on the sole basis of Christ's crucifixion and death and through the means of our genuine faith in Him.

Works, indeed, are the evidence of faith, but never its replacement, nor do works serve the same purpose. True, living and breathing faith naturally bears fruit. True, biblical faith is pregnant with works. However, once we attempt to add our good deeds as justification of our own righteousness we have "fallen from grace."[335] Yet faith that is devoid of good works is not an authentic faith. It

---

[333] Romans 4:5

[334] Romans 3:28

[335] Galatians 5:4

is a sham, a worthless religion, salt without saltiness, a fruitless tree that is cursed by the Lord.[336] And if we ever think that our good works, our obedience to any additional law, can help bolster our acceptance by God "we are deceiving ourselves, and the truth is not in us."[337]

Good works are, indeed, the consequence of belief. Just as Christ's sacrifice proved His love for the Father, so also our works are evidence of our love for God. Good works naturally stem from a branch grafted into the vine that is Jesus Christ. The fruit of the Spirit naturally flows from one siphoning living water from Christ. All of the Law's commandments are fulfilled by us when we love God with all our heart, mind, soul and strength and we love others as ourselves for "on these two commandments hang all the Law and the Prophets"[338] Love is the causation of every "thou shall" and "thou shall not" in the Law. When we love as Christ loved, we fulfill the Law, not out of resentment or even obligation but out of a consequence of His Spirit living within us. This is why "if anyone does not have the Spirit of Christ, he is not of Him."[339]

We are justified in the same manner by which Abel, Enoch, Abraham, Isaac, Jacob, David, Isaiah, Jeremiah, Rahab, Ruth and Mary were justified before God: through

---

[336] See Matthew 21:19
[337] 1 John 1:8
[338] Matthew 22:40
[339] Romans 8:9

faith. This ancient way of salvation is still alive today, and it is the sole means by which we can obtain justification. Our faith must be rooted in our trust in God rather than a trust in our self. Those who prefer a system of law by which to plant their confidence forfeit the only real means of justification. Those who would add to our yoke obedience to the Ten Commandments, or the whole Mosaic Law, preach the same leaven that corrupted the Pharisees. They, like the Judaizers then, want to trust in their own effort, their own good works, and believe that because of their own *goodness* God owes them salvation.

We, Christians, can so easily believe this same deceitful "gospel, which is not another gospel" at all."[340] We arrogantly say, *"I'm a Christian,"* or *"I go to church every Sunday,"* or *"I tithe everything I earn,"* or *"I accepted Christ as my Lord,"* or *"I was baptized,"* or *"I'm not an adulterer,"* or *"I don't drink or smoke,"* or *"I don't do drugs,"* or *"I'm not a homosexual or pedophile."* In every one of these statements the focus is on "I" and what "I" has done to merit salvation. It is no different than the Pharisee who trusted in his own righteousness. It's not that obedience to Christ or avoidance of sin is not necessary, but it is the trusting in what I did or didn't do that is fundamentally opposed to the truth of the gospel.

Anytime we place our faith, our trust in what we do, we consequently remove our faith and trust in God. Just like

---

[340] Galatians 1:6-7

those Galatian Christians who considered circumcision in order to increase their favor with God, we also can fall from the grace found in Jesus Christ. Anytime we trust in commandment keeping, we, thereby, unknowingly forfeit God's grace. "Now to the one who works, his wages are not accounted according to grace, but according to what is due,"[341] and what is due everyone who does not fully trust in the atoning work of Christ is death.

However, we, believers, are "justified freely by His grace through the redemption which is in Christ Jesus."[342] The justification available through Christ is free of charge. You can't buy it. You can't earn it. It is free. Period. "Christ has redeemed us out of the curse of the law, having become a curse on our behalf."[343] Why, oh why, would anyone want to return to the old system of death? What makes us think that once we've been saved by Christ's work we can now earn it on our own? "Having begun by the Spirit, are you now being perfected by the flesh?"[344]

However, "we will be saved through Him from the wrath."[345] Since God will render "vengeance to those who do not know God and to those who do not obey the

---

[341] Romans 4:4
[342] Romans 3:24
[343] Galatians 3:13
[344] Galatians 3:3
[345] Romans 5:9

gospel of our Lord Jesus Christ,"[346] we "having been justified out of faith...have peace toward God through our Lord Jesus Christ, through whom also we have obtained access by faith into this grace in which we stand and boast because of the hope of the glory of God."[347]

---

[346] 1 Thessalonians 1:8
[347] Romans 5:1-2

Christ can Perfect!

"For there is, on the one hand, the setting aside of the preceding commandment because of its weakness and unprofitableness (for the law perfected nothing), and, on the other hand, the bringing in thereupon of a better hope, through which we draw near to God."[348] With the death and resurrection of the Messiah, the Law was trumped. Christ's death proved the Law was ineffective to justify sinners. It was shown impotent to fight sin because of the flesh wherein sin dwells.[349] The Law could not and still cannot perfect anyone, so it was cancelled and set aside. Its use was relegated to those who need a law, "for the lawless and unruly, for the ungodly and sinners, for the unholy and profane."[350]

However, in Christ we have a better hope, a hope of resurrection, a hope of an incorruptible, sinless body, a hope of "a new earth in which righteousness dwells."[351] A new home with no tears, no pain, no suffering, and no wars because there will be no sin. A new earth that is not opposed to and subjected to sinful man because of his rebellion against his Creator.[352] A kingdom wherein God's will is fully accomplished. A new Jerusalem where our holy and righteous God sits as King and

---

[348] Hebrews 7:18-19
[349] See Romans 7:17-20
[350] 1 Timothy 1:9
[351] 2 Peter 3:13
[352] See Romans 8:20-22

exclaims, "Come, you who are blessed of My Father, inherit the kingdom prepared for you from the foundation of the world."[353]

Although the Law never perfected its adherents, God "by one offering He has perfected forever those who are being sanctified."[354] Believers in Christ are not only perfected but perfected forever. The perfection that lies in Christ is an absolute, permanent and enduring status and is granted to all those who are being sanctified, to those who continue to "walk in the light as He is in the light...[as] the blood of Jesus HIs Son cleanses us from every sin."[355]

Christ calls you to a better way wherein "you also have been made dead to the law through the body of Christ so that you might be joined to another, to Him who has been raised from the dead, that we might bear fruit to God."[356] The early church, before it was infiltrated with lovers of power, greed and lusts, understood Christ's purpose for His body. "They continued steadfastly in the teaching and the fellowship of the apostles, in the breaking of bread and the prayers...and those who believed were together and had all things common; And they sold their properties and divided them to all, as anyone had need."[357] These first disciples cared so little for their own

---

[353] Matthew 25:34
[354] Hebrews 10:14
[355] 1 John 1:7
[356] Romans 7:4
[357] Acts 2:42-45

well-being that they never hesitated when a brother or sister had a need. They just took care of it.

"Herein is love, not that we have loved God but that He loved us and sent His Son as a propitiation for our sins. Beloved if God has loved us in this way, we also ought to love one another...if we love one another, God abides in us, and His love is perfected in us."[358] This is the greatest difference between those who attempt to follow the Law and those who follow the one Teacher. The Law taught to "love your neighbor as yourself,"[359] but our Master teaches us to "love one another even as I have loved you."[360] To achieve this level of love requires a cross, a death, and a new birth. This type of love has no consideration for one's self but to solely accomplish God's will on earth.

One does not become perfect through obedience to the Mosaic Law, rather, we are perfect children when we, like our Father, do good to those who intend to do us harm. We become more like God when we are dead to our flesh, to our self-centered desires, to the old man who is focused on his own well-being, his own preservation, and his own perceived justice. We are God's children when we behave like Him, and we become more like

---

[358] 1 John 4:10-12
[359] Leviticus 19:18
[360] John 15:12

Christ, the Author of our salvation, when we are made "perfect through sufferings."[361]

Suffering is a difficult subject for many believers. Our flesh wants to believe that if we become a Christian everything will be great, but, in many cases, the exact opposite is true. The reality is: a Christian has defected from the enemy's camp and, consequently, the enemy will seek to destroy the traitor. Why do you think Job suffered the loss of his wealth, his children, and even his own health? Satan stands and accuses God's people. He argues that the only reason we obey God is because it benefits us, and the only way the Accuser can prove us wrong is by inflicting misery upon God's children.[362]

Of course, not all suffering is directly due to Satan's doing. We suffer many times because of our own choices or the choices of other free agents. We didn't choose to be born. Two other people did. We didn't choose to be robbed, slandered or even hit by a drunk driver. We don't choose that people are beat, killed, raped or sold into slavery. Again, this is the choice of others. Even physical illness can be the result of someone else's decision. When our parents, Adam and Eve, chose to disobey God and assert their own independence, God removed them from an environment of blessing. Thus, not only the ground but, all of creation is cursed,[363] and

---

[361] Hebrews 2:10

[362] See Job 1:9-11

[363] See Genesis 3:17 & Romans 8:20

because of this people hunger, people get sick, and people die.

Now, we can point our finger and accuse God all day long about how He shouldn't let us suffer, but the reality is this entire system of war, sickness and death was never His choice. He, being love, allowed man to accept the blessings He offered on the sole condition that we recognize and obey Him as God,[364] but we deemed His conditions unacceptable. In fact, every time we disobey God we prove that we are, indeed, the offspring of our parents. Just as Adam brought sin into the world, and through sin death,[365] we perpetuate this system of death when we sin, when we willfully do what we want and ignore what God desires for us.

Confessedly, I am probably not the best expert on suffering. I "have not yet resisted unto blood, struggling against sin."[366] But, as one who has faced death on a few occasions, I can tell you this: Your faith must exist prior to suffering. Faith doesn't miraculously appear because we start suffering. It many cases, suffering merely proves that our faith exists, yet this revelation does yield more confidence. But much like works, suffering vindicates the believer as having genuine faith. So if you don't have faith before you get cancer, you're not going to find it when you learn you have a few weeks to live. You won't

---

[364] See Genesis 2:17
[365] See Romans 5:12-14
[366] Hebrews 12:4

rejoice to walk in the light when the doctors explain you may never walk again. And you definitely won't trust God when your child dies of no fault of her own.

Is suffering good? Absolutely not! Why do you think Jesus was furious when he saw Lazarus dead in the tomb?[367] Jesus came to undo the works of the devil,[368] to "proclaim release to the captives, and recovery of sight to the blind, to send away in release those who are oppressed."[369] The current state of man and this world is not of God's doing, but Jesus Christ came to deliver us from this existence of sin and death. This is why we await a new heavens and a new earth.[370] This is why God promises to "make all things new."[371] Do "all things work together for good to those who love God?"[372] Yes, they do, but that good may not come on this side of Jesus' second coming. Rather, we wait on the Lord as it says, "Blessed are those who wait for Him."[373]

But how does suffering help perfect those who draw near to God? Suffering, whether it be physical, emotional, or even financial, helps subdue our flesh that wars against our spirit. This is why Paul made an effort to "buffet my

---

[367] See John 11:38
[368] See 1 John 3:8
[369] Luke 4:18
[370] See 2 Peter 3:13
[371] Revelation 21:5
[372] Romans 8:28
[373] Isaiah 30:18

body and make it my slave."[374] The flesh needs to learn submission to God's will, and the more we say, "No" to our carnal desires the less our flesh influences our decisions. And the more we retain our faith during suffering or persecution, the more we become like our Lord and Savior, Jesus Christ.

Attending church for a couple hours a week is pathetically easy, but to give up our free time to help others is a real sacrifice. Yielding a tithe when you own a huge home and have two cars in the garage is not much of an offering, but to give up anything to the poor is true spiritual worship. To not retaliate when others accuse or ridicule you is simple, but to love and pray for their salvation is the cross Jesus calls us to carry. Although our perfection before the Father is absolute because of Christ, it is through our sanctification, our struggling to become more like Him, that we begin to think, act and love like He did.

How much greater is the gospel of Jesus Christ than some rudimentary commandments that fail to even touch the garment of our gracious Master. Christ was not raised to the right hand of the Almighty or glorified above every name that can be named because He was just some great teacher. His disciples didn't gladly suffer persecution and death because He delivered some greater, esoteric ideology comparable to the Greek philosophers, the Buddha, or the later originator of Islam. He is the King

---

[374] 1 Corinthians 9:27

of Kings and Lord of Lords because He suffered and died in the stead of His enemies: sinners like you and me. He is the only king who gave His own life to save those of His enemy's kingdom. All great kings lead their warriors in battle, but only one King laid down His life for the very ones who hated Him.

This is why Paul determined to know nothing but "Jesus Christ, and this One crucified."[375] This is why he was "crucified with Christ; and it is no longer I who live, but it is Christ who lives in me."[376] This is why an esteemed Pharisee who grew up loving the Law could say, "But what things were gains to me, these I have counted as loss on account of Christ. But moreover I also count all things to be loss on account of the excellency of the knowledge of Christ Jesus my Lord, on account of whom I have suffered the loss of all things and count them as refuse that I may gain Christ and be found in Him, not having my own righteousness which is out of the law, but that which is through faith in Christ, the righteousness which is out of God and based on faith."[377]

The apostle Paul, who previously loved the Law and still loved His Jewish brethren, considered the privilege of his ancestry, the accolades from his fellow Jews, the popularity of his celebrity, the power and influence afforded his position to be complete trash in comparison

---

[375] 1 Corinthians 2:2

[376] Galatians 2:20

[377] Philippians 3:7-9

118

to knowing Jesus. And not just knowing Christ and the hope of eternal life, but Paul esteemed even more to be conformed into His image, to suffer for His name's sake, to be hated, mocked and beaten because He loved God more than life itself, more than money, more than power, more than popularity or whatever else the world could offer. He considered whatever the world could offer complete garbage.

There is nothing more fulfilling in life than "to know Him and the power of His resurrection and the fellowship of His sufferings, being conformed to His death."[378] All that the world tempts us with: temporary pleasure, financial success, fame and recognition fail miserably in comparison to truly knowing Christ. To be punished for wearing His name, to love others with a fervor that excludes any concern for self is to touch the love by which He loved us. It is this motivation that drives the one who truly knows Jesus Christ in the hopes to only here Him finally say, "Well done, good and faithful servant...Enter into the joy of your master"[379]

---

[378] Philippians 3:10
[379] Matthew 25:21

119

Conclusion

When we consider the totality of what the New Testament says concerning the Old Law and the Christian's obligation to obey it, we find that the answer is emphatically, "No." The verdict given by the council in Jerusalem coupled with the writings of Paul overwhelmingly prove that the Old Law was superseded by and with the New Law given through Jesus Christ. He, being the Sacrifice for sins, instituted a new covenant in His own blood, and He, being our High Priest, enacted a new law.

All the arguments that try to pin the old Law on believers today completely ignore the explicit statements of God's chosen spokesmen. They try to justify why only part of the law is still applicable or even "spiritualize" the believer into somehow being an Israelite and are therefore obligated to obey the Law. They ignore the plain teaching of the New Testament in order to hold on to a dead system of works. But the Bible is clear: anyone in Christ is freed from the Law.

Not only this, but this teaching does not even teach full obedience to the Law. It neglects the whole Law and arbitrarily chooses Ten as the only ones that matter. Oh, and tithing of course. How convenient that tithing is the only command outside the Ten that is obligatory. But the reality is: this position is contradictory at best. It asserts that Christians should obey the Law, but only parts of the

Law. But the Law is an all-or-nothing proposition. You either teach and obey all of it, Exodus through Deuteronomy, or you must let it go. There is no middle ground.

The old Law was replaced because it was unable to justify, free, or perfect those who followed it. Christians who are buried with Christ in baptism are buried into His death and thereby freed from the law. We are dead to the Law, and the Law is dead to us. We are freed in Christ. We are justified. We are perfected. Everything the Law of Moses was impotent to do, Christ succeeds in doing.

Anyone who teaches that a believer in Christ must obey the Ten Commandments (or anything beyond what Christ demanded) is not preaching the good news of Jesus Christ. The basis of justification is not the cross plus the Mosaic Law just as the means of justification is not faith plus works. Justification is either based upon Christ or on what good we think we've done. We either place our hope in the finished work of the cross or upon our own feeble righteousness. We cannot place our faith in the cross plus our works, even works of the Law.

The doctrine of obedience to the Law of Moses supplants the gospel of Jesus Christ. It nullifies the sufficiency of Christ's sacrifice and inherently states that God's system of grace is inadequate. When we preach this other "*gospel*," we become no more a church of Jesus Christ than is the Church of Jesus Christ of Latter Day Saints. It is a complete perversion of the good news of Jesus Christ.

Personally, when I compare the mandates of the Mosaic Law with those of Christ and of His apostles, I lose my fascination with the Old Law. The Old Law demanded a tithe; The New Law demands all of our possessions. The Old Law forbid murder; The New Law condemns hatred. The Old Law permitted lust; The New Law calls it adultery. The Old Law permitted the killing of one's enemies; The New Law demands we love our enemies. I ask you, what in the Old Law is so amazing? What in the Old Law is so fascinating? Do not even atheists keep much of the Old Law without even realizing it? Even they "show the work of the law written in their hearts."[380] But no one without knowing Jesus can truly, experientially comprehend the law and love of Christ.

But what is most troubling to me is that by teaching Christians they should obey the Mosaic Law we jeopardize their faith in Christ. When we bind on people unwarranted commandment keeping, they leave our churches in desperation, hoping they have done and will do enough to satisfy a dead system of works. Why do you think Paul was so hostile toward those who would bind on believers additional conditions for salvation? He thoroughly understood how perverse this teaching really is. And only he, a former lover of the Law, can conclude this matter better than anyone else...

---

[380] Romans 2:14-15

"It is for freedom that Christ has set us free; Stand fast therefore, and do not be entangled with a yoke of slavery again."[381]

---

[381] Galatians 5:1

Made in the USA
Middletown, DE
09 May 2018